MIRIAM'S MIDWIVES
Four Women Play Nativity

Bibliographical information by Deutsche Nationalbibliothek:
German National Library registers the original German edition of
this publication in German National Bibliography; detailed bibliographical date are accessible via
http://dnb.dnb.de.

Production and editor:
BoD – Books on Demand, Norderstedt, Germany.

ISBN: 9783746047997

1943: Young Jewess abused by Ukrainian heroes but helped by elder women.

Madonna of the yarnwinder, inspired by a lost painting of Leonardo, born on April 15, 1452 as son of a patrician with a rural worker named Catarina. Alessandro Vezzosi, founder of the Museo Ideal in Vinci, explains: "Many wealthy and prominent families bought women from Eastern Europe and Middle East. The young girls then got baptized, their most frequent names being Maria, Marta and Catarina." A fingerprint of Leonardo showed a pattern normally found only among Arabs.[1]

---

1 "Da Vinci's mother was a slave, Italian study claims." The Guardian, April 12, 2008.

MIRIAM'S MIDWIVES
Four Women Play Nativity

Six Scenes inspired by Jane Schaberg and Nilton Bonder
composed by Konrad Yona Riggenmann

A   On Historical Ground

Miriam's Midwives give a down-to-earth answer to a high-flying text that began to dominate the West as from the encounter which this same text describes as follows:

In the sixth month the angel Gabriel was sent by God to a town in Galilee called Nazareth, to a virgin engaged to a man whose name was Joseph, of the house of David. The virgin's name was Mary. And having come in to her he said: "Do not be afraid, Mary, for you have found favor with God. And now, you will conceive in your womb and bear a son, and you will name him Jesus. He will be great, and will be called the Son of the Most High, and the Lord God will give him the throne of his father David ..." Mary said to the angel: "How can this be, seeing I know not a man?" The angel said to her: "The holy spirit will come upon you, and the power of the Most High will overshadow you; therefore the child to be born will be holy; he will be called Son of God." (Luke 1:26-35)

Below the angel and the God who sent him, the text speaks rather earthly, bodily: The virgin is *afraid* of one who *comes in (εἰσελθὼν, eiselten)* foreboding she *will conceive*. She is engaged to a man but knows not a man. She doesn't get asked; there is no bit of love, let alone of lust. Something strong will *come upon* her. Since this force will *overshadow* her (ἐπισκιάσει, episkiásei) it must be a darkening force. As to fathers, two are mentioned: *David* and *God*.

With literary finesse, the Greek-encultured author around 90 CE wraps into a God-fearing story the reality of a very unhoped-for yet occurring, a scaring because dark and encroaching conception without preceding love. And all this, as Luke confirms, by order of the godly Lord to whom a woman is not entitled to object. For his contemporary Greek and Roman readers who knew Zeus & Co. as very virile godheads and like them used to have a good grip on their women, this wasn't overly offensive.

Two millennia later however the question arises which cultural side effects this primal scene had for the West. What, just for example, have the Christian depreciation of the body and of sexual nature (*natura*, the getting born), of keeping the celibate high and women low, to do with the model of the virginal obedient servant Mary?

The real weight of this primal scene however rises from the fact that the son proceeding from this scene became the paragon of obedience; that this image of his cross justifyingly accompanied the genocides on native Indians, Africans and Jews; that till this day it orients the most violent one of all continents and spreads the message of salutary, redeeming violence.

Exactly this sick message is what Miriam's Midwives face in tracing back the allegedly voluntary world-redeeming violence of Jesus' end to his beginning in his mother's womb.

Russian Madonnas, Brazilian Christmas cribs and Italian Renaissance paintings visualize this onset-to-end-violence by placing next to this child, in the manger or on his mother's lap, the cross on which the boy will die one day, according to his heavenly father's divine planning.

In light of the awful violence at the end of his short life, Miriam's Midwives should be allowed to link the Roman military violence in his killing with the one in his siring. For exactly the texts of that bible that made Miriam and Jesus world-famous also evidence that he was his mother's illegitimous child.

"My son are you, today I have begot you", God says to his Son, and he replies: "My father are you, my God."

Who gives this answer? Jesus? No, King David is this Son of God, in Psalm 2:7 (cf. 89:27). Wait a minute, says the Christian: this king David is calling God his father but in the same sense as Jesus taught us to call this God "Our father", right? But this way, dear Christian, things get even more complicated: If Jesus calls his *Abba, Father* the *Our Father*, what, then, distinguishes his sonship, his special relation to this Father from common people's relation to *Our Father?* What distinguishes his cruel sacrifice from the awful deaths of so many of *God's children*, for instance the 50,000-100,000 rebels killed on crosses during Roman occupation of Palestine or the 13 millions of Africans booked as losses on the way to the Christianized Americas or the 1,300,000 children filling fosses with their corpses because their ancestors had killed Jesus nineteen centuries ago?[2]

Let us hold that biblical texts present the son of a virgin and mother of seven (Mark 6:3) as a descendant of David as well as of God. What hides behind this Bar-Abbas triangle of a man with such strong a father-relation that Paul declared him the Son of the Most High? For now and for good measure, let's stay with Jesus Son of David,

---

2 Jews: Telushkin 2001, p.507 f.; Africans: Schützenberger, p.56.

because herefore one can take both Old and New Testament as witnesses. In nice harmony, both of them – in the gospel of Matthew which quite literally is the bridge between them – point at four immoral acts of begetting, four improperly loving great grandmothers of King David, of the Messiah Jesus, son of Miriam.

Matthew: Jesus' sinful grandmothers

"Book of descendance of Jesus Christ, the Son of David, the Son of Abraham: Abraham begot ..." and so on. This passage (Matthew 1), presenting the transition from the "Old Bible" to the "New Testament", counts down 40 old ancestors of Jesus. But scanning this congregation of long-bearded patriarchs in detail, five female headscarfs gleam among them:
"Judah begat Perez and Zerah by **Tamar** ..."
"Salmon begat Boaz by **Rahab** ..."
"Boaz begat Jobed by **Ruth** ..."
"David begat Solomon by the wife of Uriah ..." whose name was daughter of Seba, **Bathseba**. And last not least:
"Jacob begot Joseph the husband of **Mary**, of whom was born Jesus, who is called Christ" (Matthew 1, verse 16). The husband of Mary who elsewhere and doctrinally rates but as Jesus' stepfather is here the indispensable link in the genealogical chain from Abraham to Mary's son. So was Jesus begot by Joseph ben Jacob? No, for immediately after the whole chain of ancestry follows the disclaimer: "When his mother Mary was betrothed to Joseph, it happened that she, before they lived together, had conceived from the Holy Spirit" (Matthew 1, verse 18). Now not from Joseph? By whose semen, then?
Textual contradiction or careless edition? One shouldn't take Matthew, the probably only Jewish one of four gospel authors, for silly. Of course he was completely conscious of the contradiction within one and the same chapter of his text. Completely consciously he had copied the line of David's forefathers from the first book of Chronicle (1-2) and modified the line of David's offspring to get to a neat three-fold symmetry of 14 generations up to David, 14 up to Babylon and 14 from Babylon to Jesus – provided, however, that Mary is counted as a man's equivalent. Matthew's new edition is completely intentional. But what is his intention? Did he, who "writes among

9

Jews for Jews"[3] intend to appoint his Jewish readers, by introducing the four Davidian grandmothers, to an open secret in his Jewish ambience, a vital biographic detail of the fifth Jewish mother, Mary of Nazareth? What detail this might be, we can find out by taking a close look at the four uncommon women Tamar, Rahab, Ruth, Bathseba, those special mothers Matthew deemed worthy to stand in line with 40 virile patriarchs.

Tamar screws the chief: Jacob's fourth son Judah had migrated to Canaan and become the husband of the Canaanite woman Shua in mixed marriage. She bore him three sons named Er, Onan and Shelah, who grew up to – so he hoped – give Judah grandsons, and "Judah took for his firstborn Er a woman named Tamar." But Er dies early. Now the second son is obliged to marry the widow to deliver offspring to his dead and childless brother. Not very romantic, and no wonder Onan now starts to do not exactly what is termed referring to his name but coitus interruptus, every time, "and let his semen drop to earth." Because this is not healthful and "Yahve disagreed of what he did", Onan also dies. Now Tamar has to wait until Judah's third son Shelah advances up to marriagable age to be given to her as her third husband. In vain she waits. Her father-in-law Judah, meanwhile a widower himself, makes no arrangements to give his third son to his two sons' black widow. After the mourning period, widower Judah journeys to Timnah for sheep shearing. At the entrance to the village Enayim he catches sight of a veiled harlot, and for the price of a he-goat she agrees. But since he-Judah has no he-goat at hand, he asks the harlot if she will accept his signet-ring, cord and rod as pawns? Okay, she does, they do.
Three months later Judah gets alerted: "Your daughter-in-law has gone astray and become pregnant due to her sin." Well, with such a woman the chief will make short trial: "Take her out. She shall be burnt!" But the condemned young woman puts three objects in front of the patriarch's eyes: Signet-ring, cord and rod. Accused by those objective objects Judah confesses: "She's in her right against me. Why did I not give her as his wife to my son Shelah?" (Gen 38). And the child of shame and incest is named Perez and becomes one of the Messiah's great-grandfathers.

Rahab whores and helps: While Jesus' Greatgreat~grandmother

---

3 Arenhoevel et al., Jerusalemer Bibel, p.1364.

Tamar had to play the harlot just for a short time to win her case against the patron, his Great~grandmother Rahab is right in the service and probably not lacking clients in Jericho. Into this capital of Israel's enemies, two spies are sent by Joshua son of Nun. They stay in Rahab's house during the night but raise suspicions, so her compatriots ask the madam to bring forth her strange customers. They're gone already, Rahab says, but if you hurry you'll catch them! Alone again, she goes up to the roof where she has hid the two spies beneath stalks of flax. Here she begs them to swear that her father, her mother, her brothers and sisters will be treated mercifully when the city gets conquered. On a chord she lets the two James Bonds climb down out of the brothel's window, "for her house was at the city's wall (Joshua 2:15). Short time later, God's people advances to take Jericho. Joshua orders the tabernacle to be carried seven times around the walls and seven priests to blow on seven ram horns; and on the seventh day at first the walls come tumbling down and second the citizens are slaughtered.

For the walls are falling down
And the town is flattened to the earth alike
But one cheap hotel is shunned from every strike
And they ask what VIP is living there?
And this very noon there will be silence in the harbour
When they ask themselves now: Who will have to die?
And then everyone will hear me saying: All them!
And when the head drops down I just say: Hoppla!
And the ship with eight sails and fifty big cannons
Will vanish with me.

No, Rahab doesn't order "them all" to be killed and she doesn't comment with *Hoppla* as Bertolt Brecht's Pirate Jenny does. But Rahab-Jenny of Jericho, together with "her father, her mother, their brothers and all who belonged to her" is escorted from her happy house out to a "safe place" and she "remained living in Israel up to this day" (Joshua 6:25). In her new life Rahab the hooker first became an honest housewife, then a mother, grandma and Ruth's second mother-in-law. Matthew has no problem integrating the former harlot into the Messiah's maternal line: "Salmon begot Boaz from Rahab and Boaz begot Jobed from Ruth."

Ruth pulls the honest whoreson: "In the days when the chieftains ruled, there was a famine in the land; and a man of Bethlehem in Judah, with his wife and two sons went to reside in the country of Moab". The women of Moab, descending from Lot's incest with his elder daughter (Gen 19:37), are famous for their beauty. No wonder that both sons of the migrant family marry soon, the happy brides' names are Orpah and Ruth, but again both husbands die. Their father Elimelech had passed away yet before them, and his widow Naomi, having heard that in the land of Judah rain, milk and honey are flowing again, sets out to return to her people. Both daughters-in-law shed tears, "but Ruth clung to her" and insists on going with Naomi. "For wherever you go, I will go; wherever you lodge, I will lodge; your people shall be my people, and your God my God."

Arrived in Bethlehem, Ruth takes on the kind of bread-winning open to the paupers: Gleaning ears of grain on harvested fields. All by chance she comes to the field of Boaz, who all by chance just arrives from Bethlehem and asks his reapers' foreman: "Whose girl is that?" – "She is a Moabite girl who came back with Naomi", the servant tells him. "She has been on her feet ever since she came this morning and rested but little in the hut." Boaz is impressed with the Moabite belle's good references. "Don't go to glean in another field", he greets her. "I have ordered the men not to molest you. And when you are thirsty, go to the jars and drink some water of that the men have drawn." Mealtime gives occasion to get closer: "Come over and partake of the meal, and dip your morsel in the vinegar", he invites her with lavish compliments of fragrant, crispy roasted grain.

When Ruth comes home to her mother-in-law at night with amourousness beaming out of every buttonhole, Naomi asks her knowingly: "Daughter, I must seek a home for you, where you may be happy. Now there is your kinsman Boaz, whose girls you were close to. He will be winnowing barley on the threshing floor tonight. So bath, anoint yourself, dress up ..." After the early summer work peak Boaz, son of Rahab, "ate and drank, and in a cheerful mood went to lie down beside the grainpile." And so decently the Bible describes how a strong woman – all without seduction – gains her ends: "Then she went over stealthily and uncovered his feet and lay down. In the middle of the night, the man gave a start and pulled back – there was a woman lying at his feet! "Who are you?" he asks with male naivity. "I am your handmaid Ruth. Spread your robe over your handmaid, for you are a redeeming kinsman." Boaz, however, is but the second-ranking redeemer, his obligation on his distant cousin's inheritance including his widow depends from another kinsman's will. When this first redeemer renounces, due to material considerations, on the economically unsexy match, Boaz marries Ruth "and the Lord let her conceive and she bore a son. Naomi is happy, gracefully listening to the women's congratulations: "He will renew your life and sustain your old age; for he is born of your daughter-in-law, who loves you and is better to you than seven sons."

The grace of female beauty – with which Tamar was blessed maybe poorly, Rahab profession-adequately and Ruth most surely – this attraction may be found in Jesus' fourth foreign grandmother, at King David's times, in most infatuating power:

Bathseba bathes and succumbs: "The woman was very beautiful" – the young woman whom King David, strolling on the roof of his royal palace, sees bathing in another man's dominion. Spontaneously, the voyeur royale sends messengers to this cherry in neighbor's garden; spontaneously he layes with her and she – having taken this fateful bath to purify herself after her period – conceives. In order to make the fruit of love appear legitimous, David orders her husband, General Uriah, to come home from military front and almost coerces him to meet his wife. But Uriah, too ascetic or too well informed, refuses and prefers to sleep outside the gate in his troop's camp. Plan B: "Place Uriah in the front line where the fighting is fiercest", David writes to Joab. "Then fall back so that he may be killed."

And thus the angel of death meets Uriah, and David marries Bathseba, who now bears him a son. No sooner than wise Nathan tells the king a story of the "only one ewe lamb" heeded like a daughter by the poor man but slaughtered and put roasted on the table for his guest by the rich man (2 Sam 12:3), no sooner than David falls in rage against this man who "did this and deserves to die" and Nathan says: "That man is you!" – no sooner than now David breaks down, confesses, repents. Nathan, taking God's position, replies: "The Lord has remitted your sin; you shall not die" – but the child will. David fasts, sleeps on the stone floor, and ends his self-punishment no sooner than on the seventh day, when his servants dare to tell him that the baby boy has died. "Now that he is dead, why should I fast? Can I bring him back again? I shall go to him, but he will never come back to me." Then he consoled his wife Bathseba, he went to her and lay with her, she bore a son and named him Solomon.

Four Women, four questionable, but child-bearing encounters: Why did Matthew spread this four-cornered basis of Jesus' maternal ancestry before he put Mary on top of it?

University of Detroit theologian Jane Schaberg emphasizes that all four prefigurants of Mary were born non-Jewish. "Rahab and probably Tamar were Canaanites, Ruth a Moabitess, and Bathseba probably a Hittite like her husband." According to the later Jewish rule that became valid in Jesus' times and based being Jewish on being born from a Jewish mother, the four women's sons were not Jewish and nevertheless were to become Solomon's forefathers.[4] Mary, however, was a Jewess. Did Matthew want to intimate gently that this time not the mother, but the father was outlandish?

Jane Schaberg considers the four indecent women to have four common features;[5] four similarities that I, taking into account especially the perspectives of Brazilian rabbi Nilton Bonder in his book "Our Immoral Soul", will formulate with slight modifications:

1. All four find themselves outside patriarchal family structures, struggling with, and wronged or thwarted by, the male world's rules: Tamar and Ruth are childless young widows who achieve their rights by seducing elder men; Rahab a prostitute who achieves to safe her family just by her male-dominated, males-dominating profession; Bathseba is an adulteress between two warriors, and then a widow pregnant with her lover's child, advancing her lively inheritance into the center of social power.

2. In their sexual activity all four risk damage to the social order and their own condemnations.

3. All four are wronged or thwarted by the male world but achieve to turn depreciated relations with men into socially and individually positive, life conserving conditions.

4. In this task, all four are helped and their situations righted by men who acknowledge guilt and/or accept responsibility for them.

From these common features, Schaberg proceeds to the gospel writer's intentions: "Mention of these four women is designed to lead Matthew's reader to expect another, final story of a woman who becomes a social misfit in some ways; who is party to a sexual act that places her in great danger; and whose story has an outcome that

---

4 Schaberg, p.21.
5 Schaberg, p.32-33.

repairs the social fabric and ensures the birth of a child who is legitimate or legitimated. That child, Matthew tells us (1:1), is 'the son of David, the son of Abraham'."[6]

But there's a second quartet of features: One could say that the four cases of illegal begetting combine to a rather complete painting of deviant hetero-sexual encounter: Incest (Tamar), prostitution (Rahab), calculated seduction (Ruth) and adultery (Bathseba). What still misses is the most repugnant form of illegitimate sexual encounter: intercourse by force.

Sired in violence

In Joshua Sobol's drama "A Mentsh", young Sheindl enters scene with her dress tore.

Gebirtig: Sheindl? What happened?
Sheindl: Dead!
Gebirtig: What?
Sheindl: A policeman caught me at selling bagels, he dragged me
*   to an abandoned backyard.*
Gebirtig: Stop talking ... All that counts is you're alive!
Sheindl: I'm all dirty.
Gebirtig: You're all clean, Sheindl. Dirty – is he.
Scheindl: If I get pregnant, then ...
Gebirtig: I am the father. Your child is my child ...

In this case, the carpenter, poet and composer Mordechai Gebirtig is the man who helps the woman to have her situation righted; but Sheindl's situation differs from those of Tamar, Rahab, Ruth, Bathseba as basically as the case of Miriam the Nazarene. If Miriam became pregnant by a Roman act of violence, as Schaberg assumes, the features 1 and 2 do not apply to her: She did not find herself outside patriarchal structures; no civilized male world would take rape as legal; and Miriam was not active, took no risk. Quite possible or even probable, however, is that, in line with Schaberg's features 3 and 4, she, too, is helped by a carpenter in creating "life conserving conditions" out of what began with being "wronged" by the violent rules of warriors' world.

Nazareth, a warm spring day, 4 BCE. The troops marched in shortly

---

6 Schaberg, p.32-36.

before noon, two cohorts. At late afternoon, when they marched off again, fourteen women and eight girls had been raped, of whom five months later, fortunately, only three carried a Roman's child in her belly. Miriam, Joseph's fiancée, was one of them.

That's how it could have happened.

Nazareth, painted by Scottish artist David Roberts (1796-1864) in 1842.

In his Christmas play "Bariona or the Son of Thunder", French philosopher Jean-Paul Sartre has his rebel say: "Soldiers will enter our village like last year in Hebron? They will rape our women and take our animals with them?"[7]

That, too, is how it could have happened.

Historically and verifiably, what happened is this:

"It was in the period of the Roman invasion of Palestine that the Jews made an important modification in their jurisdiction. Having hitherto observed a patrilineal tradition in which rights, titles and identity were passed from father to child, Judaism at this point turned matrilineal, establishing the relations between one generation and the next one now between mother and child. In view of Judaism's strong adherence to patriarchal text tradition, there must have been very sig-

---

7   Sartre, J.P.: Bariona or The Son of Thunder. A Christmas Play, written in PW camp 1942; 2nd scene.

nificant reasons to justify such a radical amendment with this amount of implications" explains Brazilian rabbi Nilton Bonder. The shift to maternality occurred not incidentally during[8] but "just because of Roman occupation. Violent in the treatment of vanquished peoples, Roman legions were infamous for their praxis exercised already during earlier occupations: rape. For the Roman army, the power to take the nation's daughters implied the symbolical meaning to make use of this nation. The defilement of the family, the assailant expropriation of continuity, the wombs of Israel inseminated by a foreign people: this was to Judaism an all too frontal attack on survival. That those girls' wombs would present to the world the gift of sons of Rome meant more than only the looting of the present time and the erasing of the past of Israel. It meant to incorporate Israel's future."

The Jewish antidote: "Matrilinearity meant the legal solution for the status of these fatherless children of Israel and safeguarded that they would form the continuity of a people that would not submit. Particularly in the cases of rape where the children had the status of bastards, a new symbolical understanding of the situation was necessary." The problem was "children without fathers. Someone had to assume fathership for these sons who were not marginalized by any means, but contrarily represented the hope that tragedy would turn into a wonder. The task of assuming fathership would fall to no one else than God, the creator ... This is the perspective of the power of the humble ones present in Hebrew culture: the lowest one, the weakest one, the one who experienced the hardships of life most deeply is the superman actually ... Not the intact family, not correct behaviour engender the species' best individual, but the orphan, the widow, the stranger, the sick one, the whore." Moses, for instance, arose from the incorrect, incestuous marriage of Jokebed with his nephew Amram; he was saved by the disobedience of the midwives Shifra and Puah; drifted to the Pharao's daughter who disobeyed her father in pity for the Hebrew child, while this boy's cunning sister Miriam watched the rescue and hurried to recommend a very apt wetnurse – Jokhebed herself – thus closing the circle of life-saving women. Here, too, five women take part in the messiah rescue operation. "It is the woman's obligation", Bonder comments, "to preserve the semen,

---

8   Lisa Katz (judaism.about.com/od/whoisajew/whoisjewdescent.htm) claims it happened before 70 CE: "Sometime during the Roman occupation and the Second Temple period, a law of matrilineal descent, which defined a Jew as someone with a Jewish mother, was adopted."

even by employing strategies that contradict the dominant morale. In this perspective of preservation, the Messiah figures in humanity's picture album as the subversive, renegate, heretic. In all these cases [from Eve and Lot's daughters to Shifra, Puah, Jokhebed, Miriam and the Pharaoh's daughter; and from Tamar, Rahab, Ruth, Bathseba to Miriam of Nazareth] the woman, by and through her deviation, opens the path of humanity ..." To his Jewish and his many female followers, Jesus' impure, violent Roman origin may have been a well-known or even confirming fact. Being a Roman's rape son would not hinder but enhance his messianic message of non-violence, in an era of sexual violence Judaism tried to cope with by "identifying the son of *some father* as son of *The Father*" and "transforming the illegitimous son into the most legitimous". The purity of Jesus is not genetical nor is he the representant of the 'correct'. He symbolizes a possibility in which his tradition, the Jewish one, always believed: Transcending the past's violence, we'll arrive at a better world. [9]

Already before Bonder, Jane Schaberg (1938-2012) had explained the virginal conception of Jesus as patriarchal distortion and masking of the macho-real, humiliating, illegitimous making of the Godson: "The reasons for the erasure and replacement of the illegitimacy tradition are surely complex. But at base it seems to me that it could not be passed down within a patriarchal form of Christianity. Within this patriarchal structure and mindset, the illegitimate conception of Jesus was a scandal so deep, an origin so 'unfitting', that it simply had to be repressed." Starting from this basis, Schaberg arrives at a new, humanistic interpretation: "I agree that the doctrine of the virginal conception is a distortion and a mask, but I think behind it lies the illegitimacy tradition. Unmasked, that tradition presents us with fuller human realities and therefore with deeper theological potential." In bright consensus with Rabbi Bonder, the ex-nun Schaberg declares: "In this case there is a subversion of the patriarchal family structures: the child conceived illegitimately is seen to have value – transcendent value – in and of himself, not in his attachment and that of his mother to a biological or legal father. [...] The reading I have offered of the narratives as incorporating the tradition of the illegitimacy of Jesus supports and makes more precise the claim that Mary represents the oppressed who have been liberated; she becomes a symbol whose power is a power of access to reality."[10]

---

9   Bonder 1998, p.88-98 and 123-124 (italics: K.Y.R.).
10   Schaberg, p. 195-199.

Luke: Rising from humility

The perspective of low birth and highest importance, of holiness from humble origin is stressed in the gospel to which Christian folklore owes the newborn surrounded by sheep, ox and donkey. As companion of Paul, the physician Luke displays his prowess for idyllic poetry in the Christmas story with shepherds at their campfire guided by an angel to find "Mary and Joseph, and the child lying in the manger" (2:16).

Virginis partus: The virgin's birth in the first female-authored encyclopedia, the Hortus Deliciarium of Abbess Herrad of Landsberg (ca.1125-1195): Humblest possible birth (*Stabulo ponitur qui continet mundum* – In the stable is laid who contains the world) – and a young, pensative foster-father.

The highest man in lowly animals' manger: Luke's love of vertical tension helps understand what he wanted to intimate by those two contrasting conception stories he prefixed to the Christ-animal-contrast. In the first story the angel Gabriel tells the old priest Zachary that his old wife Elizabeth will conceive of him. In the second story the same high-ranking angel Gabriel deeply terrifies a young woman announcing she will conceive from on highest. Mary hurries to the mountains. But this is no post-traumatic escape from a bunch of soldiers; just "in haste" she hikes to meet her elder yet pregnant cousin, "and when Elizabeth heard the greeting of Mary, the baby leaped in her womb". And this latish mother Elizabeth

19

sings the "Magnificat", praising the one who "looked with favour on the humiliation [ταρείνωσιν, tapéinosin] of his servant"; the one who "brought down the powerful" and "lifted up the lowly". Remarkably, the word that the oldest Greek translation of the Bible (the "Septuaginta") employs here for humiliation, namely ταρέινοω ("tapéino-o", to make low, humiliate, weaken)[11] signifies in Genesis (34:2) for Dina, the daughter of Lea, as well as in Judges (19:24-20:5) for two other victims, and also in Lamentations (5:11) for the virgins of Jerusalem explicitly "the sexual humiliation of a woman".[12] Dina had gone out "to visit the daughters of the land. Shechem son of Hamor the Hivite, chief of the country, saw her, and took her, and lay with her by force" – a crime that ends in a carnage of revenge. In the book of Judges, an old resident of Gibea, in order to protect his guests by satisfying the "depraved lot" of the town, goes as far as offering his virgin daughter to the riffraff, and his guest gives them his concubine, and "they raped her and abused her all night long ..." The ensuing campaign of revenge is Homeric in its dimension.

Elisabeth's destiny is the happiest possible contrast to those rapes. In her Judean mountain village she had been called the barren one. Childlessness was commonly understood to be the woman's fault. The barren womb is spoken of as punishment for sin (Lev 20:20-21) or at least as caused by God having "forgot" the woman (see 1 Sam 1:11). Why did Luke prepare Mary's conception story by the low-high-journey of a much elder cousin? Because, explains Jane Schaberg, compared to an old wife's childlessness "the humiliation of a betrothed virgin who was seduced or raped, and who became pregnant by someone other than her husband, was far worse ... In contrast to the humiliation of the barren woman (see Isaiah 54:1-3; 1 Sam 2:5), this kind of humiliation was never explicitly promised reversal."[13] The womb of this woman humiliated by barrenness would bear the preparer John the Baptist; the birth of the cosmic redeemer from Mary's womb inescapably required a much deeper degree of previous humiliation.

Much higher value, however, Luke places on Jesus' pure and sinless pedigree: 15 generations longer than the Matthean register, mentioning David, Boaz, Perez, Juda but no woman and ending in the top three men "Seth, son of Adam, son of God". Thus Luke clarifies,

---

11 Langenscheidt's Pocket Dictionary Classical Greek – German, 1990.
12 Schaberg, p.100; cf. p.95 and 138.
13 Schaberg, p.103.

that Jesus is the son of God in the same sense as David et ceteri, in the same sense as all sons of Adam, and God could not have done anything more absurd than, kind of refreshing his own genome, to intervene anew begetting now with the fiancée of Joseph upon whom the whole ladder builds with supposed firmness in the initial verse 3:23: "Jesus, when he began his ministry, was about thirty years of age, being the son, as was *supposed*, of Joseph ..."

Mark: Jesus ben Miriam

"Your firstborn is supposed to be the son of ...": What would this sentence mean in antique or modern social context and for the addressed woman? What Mark has her Nazarene neighbors state about her when her son starts preaching in his home town is hardly less offensive: "Isn't this the carpenter? Isn't this the son of Mary and the brother of James, Joseph, Judas and Simon? Aren't his sisters here with us?" (Mk 6:3).

Since in Palestine's male-dominated society a man used to be presented in the way of "Josef-ben-Jacob" or "Simon-bar-Yona", in any case as Son-of-Father, the notion "son of Mary" is uncommon – maybe intentionally degrading, too? "There is no certain evidence", Jane Schaberg admits, that identifying a man by his mother was already in Jesus' days "a customary way of designating illegitimate children or sons of prostitutes. But it is a later Jewish legal principle that a man is illegitimate when he is called by his mother's name, for a bastard has no father."[14] German scholar Gerd Lüdemann is more outspoken: "Historically we have to conclude that the mark of Jesus as 'son of Mary' was already used against him in his home town. Thus the mark is to be termed a sneer which put the finger on a sore spot of Jesus' origin."[15]

If this home town rumour had spread until 70 CE together with the growing faith, no one has to wonder why this passage in Mark's gospel remained of all canonical pages the only occasion where the Son of God is addressed as "son of Mary". Expectably, the ensuing gospels correct the troublesome "son of Mary" in an increasing thoroughness. Matthew (13:55) amends the first gospel's text discretely, in order to identify Jesus correctly by his father: Now the people's first question "Isn't this the carpenters's son?" introduces the father

---

14 Schaberg, p.160-162; cf. Lüdemann, p.60-61.
15 Lüdemann, p.61.

so elegantly that the subsequent son-of-Mary-question becomes completely honest: "Isn't his mother's name Mary?" Maintaining the question form, Luke (4:22) fights remaining doubts by inserting the *as was supposed* father's name in a noncommittal way: "Isn't this the son of Joseph?" And the last gospel of John (6:42) has the honest family of lower middle class perfected in a slightly awkward question: "Isn't this the son of Joseph, whose father and mother we know?"

John: But you were!
Surprisingly, this last, least carnal and most spiritual gospel, written four generations after Jesus birth, in its verse 8:41 contains the most carnal allusion to the Nazarene's dark origin, in an argument with Pharisees that escalates this way: "We are descendants of Abraham" – "I know you are but ..." – "Our father is Abraham." – "If you were, you would do the works of Abraham" – "We were not born of fornication" (*Hýmeis ek pórneias ou gegennémetha*). As alien as the point-blank term pórneias is to the context, as strongly the assertation points to what remains unsaid: "... but you were!" The passage is delicate enough to produce a variety of translations: "We are not illegitimate children" (New International Version, 2011); "We of whoredom have not been born" (Young's Literal Translation); "We were not born of sexual immorality" (World English Bible). Jane Schaberg dryly resumes: "The Jews meet Jesus' challenge to their religious or spiritual legitimacy by a challenge to his physical legitimacy."[16]

Thomas: Son of the porné
In the non-canonical gospel of Thomas (whole text written ca.100-110, fragments dating back to 40-70 CE) the logion 105 has Jesus say: "He who knows the father and the mother will be called the son of a *porné*" (πόρνή, whore). Lüdemann comments: "Here Jesus speaks about himself and his special relationship to his father and mother. His statement concerning his father and his mother is literal and symbolic at the same time [and ...] obviously refers to the tradition behind John 8:41, whose content has been directed by non-Christian Jews against the procreation and birth of Jesus, imputing illegitimacy, from the beginning." The renowned gospel expert

---

16 Schaberg, p.157.

does not suppose the words of Thomas' logion 105 to relate authentic words of Jesus. "But they reflect historical facts."[17]
To these facts belongs primarily a family whose female center was the virgin-mother of Nazareth.

Her repaired family ...

Nazareth lying just 25 miles east of his home town, Palestinian Church Father Eusebios of Caesarea (ca. 260-340) wrote some things about the virgin who became a child-rich wife. His report starts in the year 62, when Miriam's second son Jacob, the "brother of the Lord" (Gal 1:19) had been executed and the Christian community of Jerusalem, which had been presided since then by Jacob, had to elect a successor: "After the martyr death of James and the soon following conquest of Jerusalem, the then still living apostles and disciples of the Lord convened with the physical relatives of the Lord, for also some of the latter ones then still were alive." Unanimously they elected as James's successor the man we heard of already: "... Simon son of Clopas, whom the gospel mentions, as apt for the episcopal see of this community. He was a cousin – so it is said – of the redeemer. For indeed according to Hegesippos, Clopas was the brother of Joseph" and "an uncle of the Lord".

Whom the gospel mentions? More precisely, it is John's verse 19:25 that unites "his mother, and his mother's sister, Mary the wife of Clopas, and Mary Magdalene" under Jesus' cross. That Clopas was Miriam's husband is confirmed also by Church Father Papias who was born around 70 and until 140 wrote extensively about oral traditions. The puzzle parts of Jesus' family fall onto their places if, according to James Tabor's view, after Joseph's early death his brother Clopas had married his widowed sister-in-law Mary in a so-called levirate marriage to "build up his brother's house (Deuteronomy 25:9);[18] when according to Tabor's convincing view, the brothers James, Joses, Judas and Simon listed in Mark 6:3 were all sons of Clopas and stepbrothers of Jesus; and if in Mark's trias of "Mary Magdalene, Mary the mother of James, and Salome" who in 16:1 together went to Jesus' tomb, this Salome was simply, naturally and

---

17 Lüdemann, p.807; I corrected his double-negation error "also gegen seine illegitime Geburt" ("that is, against his illegitimous birth") by "imputing illegitimacy".
18 Hegesippos in Eusebios, Historia Ecclesiastica 3.11; 4.22 (unifr.ch/bkv/kapitel50-21.htm; cf. Tabor, p.105; Wikipedia article "Klopas").

lovingly a stepsister of Jesus, and sister of this notorious Judas whose grandsons Jacob and Zocher (Zechariah) Eusebios, the "father of church history", honors this way:

"On Domitian's order to execute the descendants of David, according to an old report some heretics denounced the descendants of Judas, a natural brother of our Saviour, saying they were the lineage of David and relatives of Christ. Hegesippos literally relates: 'From the Lord's family still the grandsons of Judas were alive, who is said to have been a natural brother of the Lord ... [During interrogation] they replied that their assets consisted in a field of but 39 acres which they tilled ... proving by the hardness of their skin and the weals on their hands due to their arduous work that they were manual workers ... After manumission they achieved, as professors and relatives of the Lord, leading positions in the Church" which in Hans-Joachim Schoeps' reading means "congregations in Galilee".[19]

The ostracism of their grandfather started around 80. While Mark (**6:3**) counts Jesus' four brothers as "James, Joseph, *Judas* and Simon", Matthew (**13:55**) tellingly shifts him to the end: "Is not his mother called Mary, and his brothers James and Joseph and Simon and *Judas*?" In both gospels, the register of apostles (Mk 3, Mt 10) includes only one Judas, namely the Iscariot. Luke, however, and whyever, in verse 6:16 discerns literally one "Judas of James" (his brother or son?) and one "Judas Iscariot, who became betrayer" (*Ioudan Iakobou kai Ioudan Iskarioth, hos géneto prodotés*).

John provides no register of apostles. But the one who was "going to betray him" in his gospel and who in the three earlier gospels had figured as Jesus' brother and James' brother or James' son (thus Jesus' nephew), is here named the "Judas son of Simon Iscariot" (6:71), outing Mary's second husband Simon bar Clopas as a radicalist if we assume that the word Iscariot is derived from the militant "sikarii".

And Paul, the New Testament's first and founding author? He assures the Corinthians (1 Cor 15:5) that the risen Jesus first appeared to Peter, then to "the Twelve" – i.e. to all of them including Judas. Also the "Gospel of Peter" which Bishop Serapion had mentioned already in 200 CE, leaves Judas within the company. A fragment of this gospel, found in 1886 in the tomb of an Egyptian monk, ends this way: "Now it was the last day of the unleavened bread, and many were going forth, returning to their homes, as the feast was ended.

---

19 Schoeps, Hans-Joachim, p.30; Eusebios, Historia Ecclesiastica, 3:19-20. The names of Judas' grandsons mentions church historian Philip of Side (ca. 380-431).

24

But we, the *twelve* disciples of the Lord, wept and were saddened: and each one, being grieved for what had come to pass, departed to his home ...".[20]
At the end of the day, in the case of this occidental paradigm of a perfidious betrayer orthodox theologians actually have to assume four persons. All gospels have the ominous Judas Iscariot whom John (6:71) names "Judas son of Simon Iscariot"; Judas the brother of Jesus is presented by **Mark 6:3** and **Matthew 13:55**; whereas **Luke 6:15** has a Judas son of James, while the greek text has a "Judas of James", who actually was a brother of James. The fourth one is the author of the doubtlessly canonical Epistle of Judas, completing a quartet Maccoby comments with British humour: "This proliferation of Judases is itself a curious phenomenon."[21] After two millennia of persecution, also concerning this Judas Perfidias the very gospels and other well reputed sources betray a very different story of a reliable brother, a very human son of Simon Clopas and Mama Maria, grandfather of her great-grandsons and honest member of her family.

Miriam's moral advocates
North African Church Father Tertullian, himself the legal son of a Roman officer, around 197 CE mentions Jewish assertions claiming that Jesus was the son of a prostitute (Quaestuariae Filius; De Spectaculis 30:6). Tertullian, an enemy of theatre and a believer in eternal infernal torture, chilled down his rage against this slur by imagining how some day Jesus would punish the Jews for the offense: "I ... would prefer to turn an insatiable gaze on those who vented their rage on the Lord. 'This is he,' I will say, 'the son of the carpenter and the harlot ... This is he whom you purchased from Judas, this is he who was struck with the reed and fist, defiled with spittle.'"[22]
Italian Church Father Origen (185-254), who emphasized the humanness of Jesus and objected to Tertullian's teaching of eternal torture, felt obliged to reply at least to the most well-known and philosophically qualified one of those "harlot's not David's son" attacks, cited in the culture comparative work of renowned philosopher Celsus who wrote in Alexandria around 178 CE, criticizing Jews and Christians. This work's last copies were burnt after Christendom's

---

20 Maccoby 1992, p.88.
21 Maccoby 1992, p.175.
22 Efroymson: Tertullian's Anti-Judaism, p.125 (quoted by Michael, p.26).

25

establishment as state religion, but the philosopher's assertations remained preserved in Origen's polemic writing *Contra Celsum*.[23] Concerning Mary, skeptic Celsus had reported that she was "a poor country woman who earned her living by spinning". When this woman was corrupted or seduced and became pregnant by another man, a soldier named Panthera (1:69), she "was driven out by the carpenter to whom she was betrothed, since she was convicted of adultery" (1:32). Wandering forlorn, she bore her boy child secretly, writes Celsus not too different from Mohammed in his Sura 19, titled "Miriam", where she retires to a remote place and gets into labours there, a brook and a date palm helping her as kind of nature's midwives.

Origen's responses to Celsus' attacks are ambiguous. He first gives it as an opinion that "all these things worthily harmonize with the predictions that Jesus is the Son of God (1:28). He appears to accept Celsus' portrait of Jesus and Mary as outsiders par excellence, as "quintessential aliens", conceding everything but the conclusion that Jesus's claim to the title of God is unwarranted. What the spinner woman's son did not dispose of – noble ancestry, distinguished parents with the necessary means to provide their child a good formation – all this was but the dark background which made Jesus' aureole just radiate the brighter. Jesus, "with all these things against him" has yet been able to shake the whole world (1:29). His reputation is victorious over "all causes that tended to bring him into disrepute".

In 1:32, however, Origen (maybe afraid of his own courage?) sounds the counter-strike: "Let us see whether those who have blindly concocted these fables about the adultery of the Virgin with Panthera ... did not invent these stories to overturn His miraculous conception by the Holy Ghost: for they could have falsified the history in a different manner, on account of its extremely miraculous character, and not have admitted, as it were against their will, that Jesus was born of no ordinary human marriage." It is not reasonable, Origen argues, that he who did so much for the human race should not have had "a miraculous birth, but one of the vilest and most disgraceful of all" (1:33; cf. 6:73). Origen, well-known for his believe in pre-existence of souls, procedes to ask whether it weren't much more reasonable "that a soul, when being inserted into a body according to certain secret laws, will take her dwelling according to dignity and with regard

23 Giuliana Lanata (ed.): Celso. Il discorso vero. Milano 1987, p.10-13 (Wikipedia page "Kelsos"); earlychristianwritings.com/text/origen161.html.

of her former character?" Jesus' great soul, he says, "merited a body in conformity with its character; whereas a body produced by an act of adultery such as that between Panthera and the virgin would have produced "some fool" to do injury to humanity, a teacher of wickedness (1:33; cf. 6:73).

Good advocacy sounds different. Resorting to a supernatural deduction to counter the rumors about Jesus' earthly nature, Origen rather reflects than rejects the Jewish defamation that Jesus' wickedness was caused by his impure conception. According to the Toldoth, teachers played a decisive role in the personal development of this sensitive Galilean teenager, confronting him with how his body had been produced.

Toldoth Yeshu: Get out, you bastard!

"Ze sefer toledoth Adám" – this is the book of Adam's offspring": With these words begins the first verse of Genesis' fifth chapter, and already the book's title *Tol(e)doth Yeshu* appears to be a bitter Jewish irony against a nebulous rabbi whom the dubious Paul had presented as a "second Adam" (Romans 5:12). Celsus knew the Toldoth certainly, Martin Luther despised this "family history of Jesus" as a Jewish provocation, Diderot mentioned the book assertively in his Encyclopedia,[24] Pinchas Lapide recognizes in this "anti-Christian denigration" a scheme "as primitive as the embellishments in the gospels"; and nevertheless, Lapide admits that this Jewish "Story of Jesus" might date back to oral traditions of first century CE.[25]

Jane Schaberg assumes an even earlier starting point: "It is likely that the basis of the tradition does stem from the family of Jesus, probably from Mary or from the brothers or sisters of Jesus". Rumours spread rapidly, you won't retell it, in small towns like Nazareth with then, at the most, 400 inhabitants. "If the story of how and when Jesus was conceived was a family tradition, it is unlikely it would have been communicated to many. Rather, it would naturally have been kept secret. But leakage and rumor were possible, especially in the home town, and its spread can be easily imagined during the ministry and afterwards, especially on the lips of those who did not accept either the claims Jesus made or those his followers made for him."[26]

---

24 Weiss, John 1997, p.23 (Luther) and 41 (Diderot).
25 Lapide 1974, passim.
26 Schaberg, p.153-155.

Not accepted: that's exactly what, according to the Toldoth, young Yeshu was. On one side, the Nazarene teenager no doubt was a good pupil – maybe because a child's "early fright" is often "compensated by overly discipline and high performance"?[27] On the other side, alas, he obstructed his own possible normal career by blunder like lacking reverence and defiant pertness against his honorable teachers. This, too, would fit into the symptoms of an unwanted, early traumatized and verbally outcast child.

The Toldoth begins with his birth. "Miriam brought forth a son and named him *hoshua*, that is Joshua, after the name of his mother's brother. But when *kilkulo* was revealed, that is the blemish of his birth, he was called Yeshu, that is [Latin!] Jesus. And his mother gave him to a *Bes Hamedras*, that is a house of study, and he learned ... and became very wise in Torah and Talmud." Trouble was to come from the custom that among the learned scholars "neither a *Bachor* [student] ... nor a youngster" must encounter the old masters with uncovered head, "but had to stand with covered head *ki avél*, that is like mourning, his eyes fixed to the ground". One day, imagine, at the gate of the yeshiva, this intelligent pupil passed by the reverend teachers "with straight neck and bare head and did not pray for the peace of every one of them". Impertinent! When one of the scholars censures him, the pupil Hoshua even dares to raise his score by a self-willed, non-hierarchical interpretation of the scripture: "How can Moses be the greatest of all prophets if he himself asked Jethro for counsel?"

Young rebel Hoshua paid dearly for his chutzpah. "How does he make head against us?" the scholars grumble. "Let's investigate him!" By hear-say, examination and asking around, they find out some incriminating details. Mainly their colleage Rabbi Shimeon ben Shetach still knows a lot from Yohanan, the then-time fiancé of Miriam. This Yohanan, his rabbi remembers, had come to him one morning and told him what had happened to his fiancée last night: How one of her neighbors, the lascivious Joseph ben Pandera, had entered her house drunken, pretended in the darkness to be her fiancé and distressed her. Indeed she had refused: "Don't you touch me, I have menstruation." But nevertheless the deceiver had imposed his will. When later on, right after midnight, he himself, Yohanan, had knocked at his betrothed one's door also, Miriam astonishedly had replied: "This has not been your custom since the day I was

---

27 Janus, p.49.

betrothed to you, that you come twice to me in one night." Weeks later, it became visible that she was pregnant and both betrothed ones had been betrayed.

Digression to Greece: With pointed irony the Jewish authors of the Toldoth seem to have taken the motive of ambiguity error between legitimous and perfidious sexual partner from the mythical triangle of Zeus, Alkmene and Amphitryon. While the warrior Amphitryon is out on a campaign against the Taphians, his young wife Alkmene gets seduced by supreme godhead Zeus who had taken on her husband's guise. Herakles, the resulting mailman's child, in a quasi amphibian birth is born together with his twin brother Iphikles and in the end he dies, betrayed by his wife, a cruel death of sacrifice. *Anfitrião* is, by the way, until today the Portuguese word for host, and the cuckolded husband is really welcoming: He rears the two-fathers-twins together. Not so in Nazareth: Mary's ashamed fiancé, this God-fearing student Yohanan, back then had run off to far away Babylon, as Shimeon ben Shetach remembered. What's worse, now that "the shameful deed back then was made public", Miriam's half-grown son had to leave his home town Nazareth at once.[28] Expelled from school, this impurely sired *mamser* went to upper Galilee or Jerusalem, according to two different versions of the Toldoth.

The fact that Rabbi Shimeon ben Shetach lived in the first century BCE does not make the whole Toldoth unreliable. Travers Herford emphasizes the repeating figure of a rebellious student Jesus and his harsh treatment by his teachers in the few and questionable Talmud passages that mention Jesus. Reliable seems at least one Rabbi Eliezer, who said that he "conversed with a disciple of Yeshu ben Pandira". Eliezer was a pupil of Rabbi Yohanan ben Zaccai, who "must certainly have seen and heard Jesus."[29]

Panthera the panther

How come that the drunken one who speaks Aramean language good enough to be let in by Miriam in the night was known by the Roman name of a feline predator?

Christian scholars have kept interpreting "Pantera" as a bowdlerized Greek "pártenos" (virgin), i.e. a Jewish attack against virginal conception – though yet in 1859, Rhenanian construction-workers had

28 Callsen et al., p. 41-49.
29 Travers Herford, p.52-53 and 352.

come across a stone-hard evidence: a tombstone for a Roman soldier, with the effect that the theological virginization of Pantera "will no longer hold up".[30] For here was chiselled, with a tool of first century CE, the very name mentioned by Celsus, by the Toldoth and the Talmud in the second to fourth century.

Jane Schaberg resumes the present state of knowledge: "Panthera was a common Greek proper name, found in many Latin inscriptions of the early Empire, especially as a surname of Roman soldiers. An inscription found on an epitaph in Germany, for example, mentions a Sidonian archer, Tiberius Julius Abdes Pantera, who was transferred in 6 C.E. from Syria."[31]

Just five miles distant from Nazareth, the antique Hellenic city of Sepphoris (Zippori) was destroyed by Roman troops in 4 BCE in response to an insurrection led by Judah ben Hezekiah against the pro-Roman Herodians after Herod the Great's death. Historians Horsley and Silberman shed light on the fall of Zippori:

In March of 4 BCE, the Rome-dependent 69-year-old King Herod, having never been accepted by many Jews due to his Idumenean origin, had succumbed to his long-term illness. His son and successor Archelaos reacted to the immediate uprises with all hardness. His cavalry slaughtered thousands of temple pilgrims in Jerusalem at Passover time. But when the news of the Jerusalem rebellion spread, messianic leaders in all regions rose up, each one hoping to be proclaimed the new king. Rebel nests formed in Judean villages.

"In Galilee, a certain Judah, son of a famous gang leader executed years before by Herod, led his followers in a raging attack through the streets of Sepphoris, invaded the well-sorted arms depot and took treasures as well as luxurious furniture out of the governor's palace. The Romans reacted with expectable hardness. Syrian governor Quinctilius Varus set out immediately with two legions southward, supported by the mobilized armies of the Hellenist cities and the other loyal princes of the region. In autumn, the Roman army had already combed out many of the country's cities and villages, raping, killing and destroying almost everything that came to their eyes. In Galilee, the centers of rebellion were suppressed brutally; the rebel-held city of Sepphoris, burnt down and all surviving inhabitants sold into slavery."[32]

---

30 Nicholls, p.14.
31 Schaberg, p.167.
32 Horsley/Silberman, p.18-20 (cf. Carroll, p.83).

Thus Roman commander Publius Quinctilius Varus extinguished the rebellion with blood, crucifying 2000 Jews all over Palestine. Having flattened Zippori and defeated the Jewish rebels, he was to suffer his own defeat 13 years later in Germania's dark forests. Would Panthera, well in his thirties, now run escaping from fierce German warriors instead of raping Jewish girls? Could Jesus' father have survived the defeat of three legions healthy enough to continue serving the army, drinking Rhine and Moselle wine, to die at age 62 and be buried with military honors? Does it matter whether he merited this honors or if, by strange coincidence, just he among the hundreds of Panteras in Roman legions (yet in 1906 Adolf Deißmann confirmed 6 Panteras but in first century CE) had been the father of this Jesus he never knew?

Anyhow, James D. Tabor[33] can itemize some indices that confirm at least the Pantera hints of Celsus and Rabbi Eliezer:

• Epiphanios (~320 – 403), this zealously orthodox bishop born near Beit Guvrin south of Jerusalem, ascribes a certain credibility to the Jesus-ben-Pantera tradition, however viewing "Jacob Panthera" as Jesus' grandfather.
• Abdes is the latinized form of aramaic *ebed*, signifying "servant of God"; the surnames Tiberius and Julius are *cognomina* he acquired in later years, giving evidence that he was not a Roman citizen by birth, but maybe a released slave who was given citizenship by emperor Tiberius, due to his military service.
• His Libanese home region of Sidon (to which Jesus made a short visit according to Mark 7:24) is situated less than 50 miles from Sepphoris and 60 miles from Nazareth;
• His cohort of archers was transferred in 6 CE to Dalmatia and 9 CE to the region between the river Rhine and affluent river Nahe.

Anyhow, Nazareth and Mary were within one historical focus of Roman rape raids. Tabor's Panthera theory does not explain how the victim got notice of the rapist's name. Maraudeurs don't use to be great narrators. Still, the Lebanese legionary spoke Mary's language; his comrades could have called him by his name; as a standard bearer he would have been the second most important soldier of his unit after the centurio and at least at parades would dress a predator's skin;

---

33 Tabor, p. 86-94; Adolf Deißmann: Der Name Panthera. In: Orientalische Studien, Gießen 1906, p.871-875 (quoted by Tabor, p.429 and his website).

maybe he had been infamous already in the small village of some hundred families. The Bingerbrück Pantera surely was acquainted if not with Mary, so with the region, and looked back to a long life in the Legion, when he, shortly after the legion-crucified Son-of-Man, shut his eyes on father Rhine's western embankment.

Left and center: Tombstone found near Bingerbrück on Rhine, where a bridge over tributary river Nahe had existed yet when Bingen was Roman Bingium.The inscription reminds TIBerius JULius ABDES PANTERA [from] SIDONIA, [died] ANNO LXII [62 years old], STIPENdio XXXX MILITIS [in service since 40 years], EXS [Exsignifer, former standard bearer?], COH I. SAGITTARIORUM [cohort I of archers]. H·S·E [Hic Situs Est, here he lies].

Right, location Bonn, 60 miles north of Bingerbrück: The tombstone of another signifer, named PINTAIVS PEDILICI/ F(ilius), depicts the standard bearer dressed in a predator's skin, the animal's head covering his helmet and its fore-paws crossed upon his breast. Inscription: ASTVR TRANS/ MONTANVS CASTEL INTERCATIA (Asturian from trans-Pyrenees fortified city Intercatia) SIGNIFER C(o)HO(ortis) V ASTVRVM (standard bearer of 5th Asturian Cohort), ANNO(rum) XXX STIP(endiorum) VII (37 years of service), H(eres) EX T(estamento) F(aciendum) C(uravit): Heir had (this tombstone) crafted according to contested will.

Strange coincidence, if Jesus' father would have died and been buried

32

exactly in the land where later Martin Luther sighed in a table talk: "The destruction of Jerusalem was cruel and lamentable. But even for God it was too much to see his only son crucified outside of town."[34] Stranger coincidence, if this son's carnal father, a rapist and crucifier of rebels, lay buried exactly in the land where the destruction of the Jewish people was planned and performed with all the lust for just punishment that the crucifixion of the innocent had aroused for thousand years.

Lapide supposes that also Judas' uncle (Clopas' brother) Joseph had died on the cross of rebels. "We cannot exclude that Joseph belonged to those pious partisans who joined the liberation movement of Judas the Galilean until General Varus scattered them, destroyed their houses und had 2000 of them crucified – when the son of Joseph was still a boy."[35] In my view, we cannot exclude any better that Mary in those terrible years – Varus raged in 4 BCE – was traumatized twice by the Romans who raped her and took away her fiancé. Double reason for Joseph's brother Clopas to marry her and become the father of the children who are counted by their Nazarene neighbors in **Mk 6:3**: "Isn't this Mary's son and the brother of James, Joseph, Judas and Simon? Aren't his sisters here with us?" Also David Flusser assumes that Joseph died early, "maybe he died when Jesus was still very young". The Jewish historian states that there "seems to have existed a certain tension between Jesus and his family." Apparently, this psychological fact "whose reasons we don't know" had effected a certain influence on his personal and "for mankind so highly important decision".[36]

In search for the reasons why the son so foolhardy risked – or subconsciously seeked – crucifixion, we have but one source: his proper statements about himself.

Telling words of an intruded child

In 1993 the Canadian theologist William Nicholls noted: "Even if Jesus was actually conceived as the son of a Roman soldier, especially as a result of rape or seduction, that would not make him illegitimate by Jewish law, since he was born of a Jewish mother and

34 Isaac, p.290.
35 Lapide 1988, p.99-101.
36 Flusser, p.23.

not as an offspring of adultery or a prohibited marriage."[37] When one year later Nicholls' colleague Jane Schaberg defended the thesis that Jesus probably was the result of rape suffered by Miriam, she hardly could have exposed herself in a more lonely way within predominantly male theologian circles. One of the few colleagues who dared to stand by and protect her was Donald Capps:

"What I believe is occurring here is a not-so-subtle form of verbal shaming. Schaberg is being told by her colleagues in the field of New Testament that she crossed a line that she ought not to have crossed, that, in fact, she has committed a shameful act. Her critics undoubtedly miss the irony here, *for this is precisely* what her book is about: the shaming of a woman and the power of a patriarchal system to protect its own interests."[38]

And not too unprecisely this is the verbal form of what Roman warriors – in Schaberg's and my view – did to Miriam physically. What this meant mentally for the collaterally produced children is a question that could be answered by thousands of children who meanwhile are adults in Bosnia: living souvenirs of modern khaki and Kalashnikoff Pantheras, of machos who had applied "single, group and continuous rape"[39] as defiling means of ethnical cleansing. Those happy ones of these forced-into-being babies who had not been killed soon after birth were raised, according to a UNICEF study, as a "particularly vulnerable ... hidden population", either in children's asylums or "at home" by their mothers. "In one family, the child was coerced to comprehend his life as a mistake" and had to present himself to guests confessing: "I am the product of my mother's violation."

In the 2004 war movie "A Boy from a War Movie", Alen Muhic is shown playing cheerfully with his classmates and scrambling with his adoptive father, and he also tells how he got knowledge of his real origin from a talkative classmate, how he ran to his "father" immediately and how this honest man told his adopted son the truth. What the movie does not render is Alen's hurt when the neighbors suddenly called him "Pero" – a Serbian name – and how he desperately tried to meet his mother, who however rejected him roughly.

What the movie does not tell is "Pero's" attempt to commit, because of this rejection and the ongoing classroom mobbing, suicide.

---

37 Nicholls, p.15.
38 Capps, p.125 (italics: K.Y.R).
39 Classification by Human Rights Watch, quoted in: "Sie wollten uns zerstören, aber wir haben überlebt", SZ-Magazin, Süddeutsche Zeitung, 10/2013.

What is not shown is how he for several days kept crying and rioting at his adoptive parents' home. "Why have you deceived me?" he shouted at his foster mother. "You said you've carried me here!" and pointed to her womb.[40]

To the adoptive mother's womb, to note, the non-raped one. And what do the victims feel? Nothing traumatizes deeper than rape, psychologists declare. "The victims mostly perceive the crime not as sexual action but as an extreme and abasing form of violence against their person and body, linked with strong fear of death", Regensburg military sociologist Ruth Seifert writes.

"They wanted us to bear Serbian babies" Enisa says. "They wanted to destroy us. But we survived." The International Criminal Court of Den Haag declared the rapes as military tactics. The rape tacticians knew how men are wired. "In every domestic quarrel my husband reproaches me with having let rape happen", Amra says. "When we married he told me that it's not my fault and he could live with it. But he can't. Asmira found a female doctor willing to abort the child. During the first post-war years she thrice attempted suicide and frequently was in psychiatric care.

In 2011, Angelina Jolie produced her film *In the Land of Blood and Honey* with solely local actresses and actors. "The women in Bosnia are glad about this film", Enisa states. "I don't hate the Serbians. They've been my neighbors, one of them arrested me, one of them saved me. But what I can't suffer", Enisa says, "is people saying don't make such a fuss, it's so long gone all that. Reconciliation can happen only if people recognize that these things happened and that the impacts of those deeds persist."[41]

What kind of relation can a woman who has conceived in this traumatic way develop to *her* and the rapist's child? If we trust the Toldoth narrative that her son's good school education was important to her, Miriam did not reject him, and not at all roughly. Apparently she loved him and stood by him, in spite of the evil primary memories. But how did he, her son, experience the time between conception and birth, while his small body grew from two to two trillion body cells? Modern science has proved with stringent evidence that already embryos perceive their mothers' feelings; that all of us yet since

---

40   George Jahn, AP: "Leben mit der grausamen Wahrheit", in: Südwestpresse Ulm, May 25, 2005.
41   Ruth Seifert, Enisa, Amra, Asmira (and Yael Danieli, p.94) in "Sie wollten uns zerstören, aber wir haben überlebt", SZ-Magazin, Süddeutsche Zeitung, 10/2013.

the act of procreation carry within us the vitally decisive judgement whether we are welcome or rejected, invited or intruded; the judgement that will model the process of our life.[42] Having grown for nine long months into this "rejecting womb",[43] as literally *em*-pathic, *in*-feeling inner listeners to their mothers' frights, complaints and heartbeats, as *part*-takers of all that she is forced to gulp, undesired children start to show conspicuous behaviour as soon as they are born. At this stage, one third of their mothers regret to have foregone aborting what has grown inside them.

Many parents of unwanted children are inclined to ill-treatment "out of rage and helplessness" – or to overcare their children in order to compensate for self-reproaches after intermittently intensive feelings of hate. Among their classmates, the unwanted ones often go for "deviants" or "cowards" and, contrarily, as daringly go-aheaded. Grown up, the unwanted ones suffer permanently of relational problems, are social misfits, twice as often criminal and not rarely lifelong incapable of happiness.[44] They tend to alcohol and drug abuse, but also to life-endangering sports like skydiving or motorcycling, this being no surprise considering their generally higher rate of suicide. Ultrasonic scans of modern days can visualize – as US-scientist Jeanette di Pietro proved – the little in-belly-human's distinct reactions even to such trifles as encumbering thoughts passing through the mind of the "surrounding" mother.[45]

How should children not perceive those encompassing emotions? How would undesired fruits of the womb try to understand their superfluous existence? How many cumbering thoughts had passed through brain and heart and belly of a rape-impregnated girl of Nazaret? How many of those thoughts and tears and sighs and cries had her baby overheard, and how did they inform his later feeling, acting, speaking out?

Every child, writes Francoise Dolto, is obliged to put up also with the scars of his mother; "he carries this debt contracted during his prenatal fusional period." From the fact that "*in utero*, as early as the seventh month of pregnancy, the child begins to dream", Anne

---

42   Häsing/Janus, p.117.
43   cf. Kafkalides, Athanassios: The Knowledge of the Womb. Heidelberg 1997 (quoted by Janus, p.17).
44   Feature "Ein Leben lang unglücklich", Augsburger Allgemeine ca. 1991; cf. the studies of Gerhard Amendt and Michael Schwarz, as well as Czech and Swedish studies described in Janus, p.111-112.
45   Alberti, p.76.

A.Schützenberger concludes that the mother "could be transmitting her dreams to her child" while the unborn could have access to her unconscious.[46]

On the other side, traumatized mothers can give their children forces with a vengeance. A two-phase study of Alexandra Piontelli with pregnant women and their then born children showed: "A mother's fantasies, hopes, and emotions for a fetus in the womb affect the infant's coming into the world and modalities of being."[47]

So mothers yet prenatally give orders to their children? In his Fate Analysis, Leopold Szondi writes that "every human being comes to this world with a life plan which under guidance of hidden inherited elements determines our fate-forming actions of free choice unconsciously." Szondi does not deny free will in making those choices, but he endeavors to prove "that fate, whether it manifests by choice in love and friendship, in profession, form of disease or mode of death, is always choice, because: choice makes fate."[48]

Is this true also for Jesus' life and fatal end?

During the 1970s, German rallies for legal abortion used the darkly intuitive rhyme "If Mary'd done abortion, she'd spared Him gruesome portion." We can try to intuit the feelings and motives of Him who was spared nothing only out of what He most probably really said, passing all the words He is said to have said through the filter of a rigid historical criticism. Just fifteen percent of all gospel-words eventually pass through Gerd Lüdemann's sequence of seaves as authentic words of Jesus (marked by bold font in this book). This extract of what Jesus carried inside and spoke out is like scattered shards of a broken vessel, enabling us to compare the vessel's engravings with the scars disclosed by children of later times and mothers. I will classify this emotional patchwork according to three relations: to life (acceptance, confidence, joy of being); to sexuality; and to father.

1. Life. Alfred Adler wrote in 1937: "The child should perceive his entrance into the world as a kind invitation. A child who doesn't feel kindly invited, lives like in a foreign country."[49] A child like this "cannot arrive at the other ones", American therapist Barbara Findeisen said in 1997; this child "can't find a place on earth ... and cannot

---

46 Schützenberger, p.32 (Dolto) und 145.
47 Piontelli, From Fetus to Child, London 1992, p.1-25 (quoted by Schwab, p.141).
48 Szondi, p.20-26.
49 Levend/Janus, p.112.

settle down". Nests and caverns are archetypes of prenatal comfort for discomforted ones.

> *"Foxes have dens and birds have nests, but the Son of Man has no place to lay his head."* (**Mt 8:20; Lk 9:58;** **Thomas 86:1-2**)

Barbara Findeisen speaks about the "melody of life" we learn in the womb. If this melody whispers only *piu triste* and *ritardando* because what lacks is the feeling of being welcome, the weakly connected ones "will be rather shy in their relationships". Since any separation recalls the child's pain of feeling abandoned, any later lovelornness "mixes with the whole despair of the child we once have been"; of a child who for all his life will nevermore "obtrude" on someone, be nobody's "burden" any more – as this child once had perceived to be in a harbouring-rejecting body.[50]

> *"When his family heard it, they went out to restrain him, for people were saying: 'He has gone out of his mind'"* (**Mk 3:21**)

Frequently, the unwelcome intruders bear "a feeling of guilt of having been born at all". In his essay *The Unwelcome Child and his Death Impulse*, Sandor Ferenczi wrote: "The child must, by immense amounts of love, tenderness and care, be induced to excuse the parents for having him brought to this world; otherwise, soon the destructive drives will stir." Destroying what? "In later life", Ferenczi notes concerning two patients, "relatively trifling occasions were enough to want to die, even if this was compensated by strong efforts of will. Moral and philosophical pessimism, skepticism and disconfidence became their conspicuous traits of character."[51]

> *"If anyone comes to me and does not hate father and mother, wife and children, brothers and sisters – yes, even their own life – such a person cannot be my disciple."* (**Lk 14:26**)

---

50 Cf. Janus 2000, passim; Findeisen, B. in her article about long-term psychic consequences of pre- and perinatal experiences, in: Janus, Ludwig and Haibach, Sigrun (ed.): Seelisches Erleben vor und während der Geburt, Neu-Isenburg 1997.
51 Ferenczi, p.253-254.

The Latin verb *linquere* means to leave back, desist from, abandon; and often this feeling of being left back and abandoned ends in the delinquency of a "disoriented" adolescent.[52] Responding to his feeling of being left, he tends to leave the patriarchal order. Miriam's son, for instance, defied the teachers of tradition and was put outside of traditional order, "outed" by them as a "*mamser*" (bastard). Should anyone be surprised if the intelligent thoughtful teenager would be uncertain about his identity, asking:

> *"Who do people say I am?"* (**Mk 8**:*27***-29**)
> *"But you? ... Who do you say I am?"* (**Mt 16:15***)*

If a mother rejects her pregnancy, she shuts herself off from moments of joy and joyous anticipation. Biochemically, she and her child will lack the "hormones of joy", serotonin and oxytocin. What her mind lacks at the moment, and maybe her child will lack for all his life is the feeling of the "world's rightness"[53]. Such persons often are very thin-skinned, feeling to be "too permeable, too unprotected in their essence, oversensitive and delicate". Searching for the roots of their being different, they become introspective – and keep contact with their "inner child":

> *"Whoever doesn't receive the kingdom of God as a little child will never enter it."* (**Mk 10:15***)*

2. Sexuality: Would it be astonishing if a rape-conceived child should develop an "unbiological sharpness ... against man's sensual desire" as historian Will Durant (married almost 70 years to his former student and co-author Chaya Kaufman) observed in Jesus?[54]

> *"But I tell you that anyone who stares at a woman with lust for her has already committed adultery with her in his heart."* (**Mt 5:28***)*

If, according to the already quoted studies of Alexandra Piontelli, "a mother's fantasies, hopes, and emotions for a fetus in the womb affect the infant's coming into the world and modalities of being",

---

52 Alberti, p.72.
53 Alberti, p.31 and 103; in German: "Richtigkeit der Welt".
54 Durant, p.638.

would it come as a surprise if this child emphasized women's rights against irresponsible, abandoning men?

> *"Anyone who divorces his wife and marries another woman commits adultery against her."* (**Mk 10:11**)

And if to him sexuality remained connected with the womb-feeling of a young girl who had been impregnated violently?

> *"For there are eunuchs who from the mother's womb were so born."* (**Mt 19:12**)

3. Father: What answer should we expect, if the force-made father-less one is solicitated by one of his activists: "Sir, permit me to bury first my father"?

> *"Follow me, and let the dead bury their own dead."*
> (**Mt 8:22; Lk 9:60**)

Should we be surprised if this son, in sharp contrast to this negative image of a "father, bad, gone somewhere" (but all too present in the Roman occupators) would develop a contrasting, consoling image of a "father, good, caring, responsible, up there"?

> *"Father in heaven, may your name be kept holy."* (**Mt 6:9** *and* **7:11;** **Lk 11:2** *and* **11:13**)
> *"So if you who are evil know how to give good gifts to your children, how much more will your Father in heaven give good things to those who keep on asking him!"* (**Mt 7:11**)
> *"But your heavenly Father already knows all your needs."* (**Mt 6:32;** **Lk 12:30**)

What will an unwanted child undertake who grew up with feelings of alienation and homelessness in this world, yearning for the homey sheltered safety he missed yet in the womb?

> *"I will set out and go back to my father ..."* (**Lk 15:18**)

Wouldn't this fatherless child dream of a father who cares just for this one lost child more than for hundred safe ones and who will come certainly to get him out of here?

> *"Suppose a man has 100 sheep and one of them strays. Won't he leave the 99 sheep in the hills to go on searching for the one that has strayed? And if he finds it, I tell you the truth, he will rejoice over it more than over the ninety-nine that didn't wander away! In the same way, it is not the will of your Father in heaven that even one of these little ones should perish."*
> **(Mt 18:12-14; Lk 15:4-6)**

All those gospel-words of Jesus speak of the same sufferings and symptoms unwanted children relate until today. All put together, those puzzling word-protocols of the synoptic gospels, presenting Jesus as his family's misfit and enfant terrible – all these words are badly fitting a perfect heavenly father but perfectly a bad primal scene in Jane Schaberg's and my view. All these words Gerd Lüdemann assigns as authentic, and as authentic are the symptoms they point to and the more valid is the thesis of Jesus' origin having been violent. "I cannot think of any need in childhood as strong as the need for paternal protection", writes the same Sigmund Freud who states that "the origin of the religious attitude" incontrovertibly can be traced back to "the infant's helplessness and the longing for the father aroused by it."[55] On grounds of this "longing for the father", US-theologian Donald Capps is right in a very deep sense when he, "against the tendency to minimize the impact of childhood experience", propounds the total anti-thesis "that virtually everything that Jesus said and did as an adult is traceable, in one way or another, to his awareness of being an illegitimate child". This awareness could explain "what is commonly judged to be the core of his own religious experience and public message, his unusually close and personal relationship to God whom he called 'my father'."

"Would it be merely happenstance", Capps asks, "that an illegitimately conceived child, a child raised by an adoptive father, not only addressed God as father, but did so in an unusually intimate manner?" And more exactly, in a very personal, idiosyncratic manner which is "diametrically opposite to his perception of his natural father"; in a

---

55   Freud 2010, (Civilization and Its Discontents), p.25.

strident and world-historically important case of "image-splitting"?[56] In a surreal scene, reported in all synoptic gospels (Mk 5:1-17; Mt 8:28-34; Lk 8:26-39) Jesus asks a demon-obsessed man for his name. "My name is legion", the madman replies, "because there are many of us inside this man". And the legionary's rape-son commands the whole legion of demons into an absurd herd of two thousand pigs – the epitome of impure, foreign, sexually uninhibited beings. This crazy fantasy suggests that Mark personally knew more than he reveals in naming Jesus the son of Mary; enough about Jesus' gentile, legionary, sexually impure origin to be able to perceive what was "inside this man" and to see what Capps would see much later: "His 'pathology' is that he has the genes of a Roman, and is therefore occupied by a foreign element that can only be exorcized by replacing this inner demon with a new internalized father, the one he affectionately calls 'my father'."[57]

The image-splitting is bipolar: the more violent, careless and abandoning this father of back then, the more worth confidence, the more helpful and sincere the father of the future would have to be. Just believe strongly. Faith can move mountains and remove bad fathers. "His awareness of his illegitimacy and his deeply personal experience of God as father ... would enable him to transform the self-endangerment caused by his illegitimacy into a new sense of self-empowerment and inner freedom, one that challenged the negative self-image resulting from awareness of his illegitimacy."[58]

Jesus' father-image-splitting would result in a split duality of his biographic options. First, the illegal Alpha of paternal violence would be followed by the high Omega of paternal help: Legion pigs would run mad to drown themselves in the Galilean sea – whereas the son of humiliation would, see Psalm 136:12, be raised to power by father's strong hand and outstretched arm! Second, the brilliant student of the scriptures, as the Toldoth describes him, must have studied Isaiah's anti-hero, God's suffering servant: "I will give him the honors of a victorious soldier, because he exposed himself to death. He was counted among the rebels. He bore the sins of many

---

56 Capps, p.108-115.
57 Capps, p.120; Schützenberger (p.76), citing her colleague Jean Guyotat, notes that "when difficulties occur on the level of instituted filial relationship – an illegitimate child, uncertainties about the father ... it weakens the instituted axis and tends to exalt the imaginary axis in a kind of dialectic relationship between the two."
58 Capps, p.108-109.

and interceded for rebels. "Sing, O childless woman, you who have never given birth! Break into loud and joyful song, O Jerusalem, you who have never been in labor. For the desolate woman now has more children than the woman who lives with her husband,' says the Lord." (Isaiah 53:12-54:1 in King James/New Living Translation). High-flying Isaiah would suit well as Jesus' favorite prophet, most deeply maybe in his verses 49:1-5: "The Lord appointed me before I was born, he named me while I was in my mother's womb ... And now the Lord has resolved, he who formed me in the womb to be his servant, to bring back Jacob to himself ..."

Already when his nerved teachers called him a *mamser* from the womb, the boy whom his mother had named *hoshua*, that is *(God)-will-save* could refer the passage of God-wanted passion for the liberation of many and intercession for rebels to himself. Twice seven years later it erupted from the man who had to say to himself: "My semen is legion."

A case of literally self-fulfilling prophecy?

No, this is nonsense, the famous Jerusalem scholar Joseph Klausner might comment. In his view, the gospels contain "not even the faintest indication concerning heathen blood rolling in Jesus' veins ... The truth is, that Jesus, like every other child in Galilee, descended from honest Jewish parents, for also in this province betrothed girls were supervised sternly, if perhaps indeed not all as strictly as in Judaea."[59]

The psychological truth is that Klausner's idyllic view, completely alien to Jesus' visibly traumatized personality, rather exemplifies Lüdemann's statement that "theological interpretation on golden ground is one thing. Another thing is the partly brutal history in this earth's dust that Jesus came to know in boosted amount. Since his appearance in his home-town Nazareth he was attacked referring to his being a bastard without legal father; hence the scorn-word 'son of Mary'... Maybe herein consists one root of his later concern for despised people, for whores, tax collectors, sinners ..."[60]

While this concern for despised women is highly regarded by Christians, the exposure of its root – Jesus' coming into this world by a violent sexual act – is utterly inacceptable to many Christians. At least on first glance. On second glance they could detect that this lowest possible way of getting sired, while not doing any harm to

---

60 Lüdemann, p.879-880.

the human dignity of the man who emphasized the human dignity of whores, thoroughly fulfills the criterion "he humbled himself" (Philippians 2:8), realizes it much more authentically, incarnates it, brings it to this planet much more physically than Luke's child in the monger between animals, since "God chose what is low and despised in the world" (1 Cor 1:28). And this humblest possible origin not even contradicts the God-sonship of Jesus Bar Abbas if one lends an ear to Paul, in Romans 8:15: "When we cry, 'Abba, Father!' it is that very Spirit bearing witness with our spirit that we are children of God."

Jesus Bar Abbas

In his documentary film "Shoah", producer Claude Lanzmann interviews, on the holiday of 'Mary's Birth', a group of Polish Catholics in front of their new-gothic church in Chelmno where from December 1941 to spring 1943 and again from June 1944 to January 1945 the Jews, after a night in church, had entered the Vergasungswagen. Now 40 years later, the only survivor Simon Srebnik has come back from Israel to stand here amidst his old friends and playmates of childhood. When Lanzmann asks them: "What do you think why this could happen to the Jews?" forward steps one Mr. Kantarowski who then had given "bread and cucumbers" to the Jews. Energetically he tells a story in which a rabbi – with the SS-officer's permission – had explained to his waiting community how, long time ago, the Jews had condemned Christ, who was completely innocent, to death and said his blood shall come upon us and our children. And now, the rabbi said, this time has come, "so let's do what we're required to, let's go!"

Lanzmann: "Ah, the rabbi has said this!"

Kantarowski: "When Pilate washed his hands he said: 'This man is innocent, I don't want to have to do with this story', and he sent Barabbas. But the Jews shouted 'His blood shall come upon us!'"

Short significant silence.

Then Kantarowski: "That is the end, now you know everything."[61]

Did Mr. Kantarowski know that his name, probably derived from the cantor of a synagogue, pertains to 212 victims listed in the memorial of Yadvashem, Jerusalem? Now let's go back to there: What do we know about Jesus' defender Pilate, Jerusalem's noble Roman gover-

---

61   Lanzmann, p.17-19 and 132-137.

nor, and what's more, canonical saint of the Coptic Church?

Having condemned Jesus at some day amidst of his term of office, in 36 CE Pilate triggered his own dismissal by his last and bloodiest massacre, which sheds light backwards on his Gethsemane to Golgotha schedule:

At Mount Garisim, the holy site of Samaritans, a group of Samaritans had been persuaded by a preacher to ascend the mountain in order to see sacred artifacts allegedly buried there by Moses. Pilate sent in "a detachment of cavalry and heavy-armed infantry, who in an encounter with the firstcomers in the village slew some in a pitched battle and put the others to flight. Many prisoners were taken, of whom Pilate put to death the principal leaders and those who were most influential."[62] In their complaint filed with Vitellius, the Governor of Syria, the Samaritan council of elders avered that they had gathered at Garisim "not to revolt against the Romans but to escape the violence of Pilate". When Pilate was ordered back to Rome to give report about this clampdown, his files were already filled with what his contemporary Philo notes apart from his character traits ("vindictiveness and furious temper ... naturally inflexible ... a blend of self-will and relentlessness") and what was intolerable for Roman reputation as a state founded on law, namely "the briberies, the insults, the robberies, the outrages and wanton injuries, the executions without trial constantly repeated, the ceaseless and supremely grievous cruelty."[63]

During his ten years term of office Pilate had sent about 6000 Jews to crosses.[64] That means, just doing business as usual he at an average made 11 men per week croak on the cross. His own condemnation Pilate is said to have evaded by suicide.[65] Not even this end did impede his veneration by the Coptic Church, whereas the Greek Orthodox Church sainted his first lady Procula who seems to have been sleeping well before her husband's normal workdays but had cautioned him against this very special one among his 6000 crucifixions: "Have nothing to do with that righteous man; for last night I suffered a great deal because of a dream about him" (Mt 27:19).

Amidst these thousands, the condemnation of Jesus had been nothing but "an insignificant act of police", as theologian Maurice Goguel

---

62 Josephus, Antiquities of the Jews 18.4.1.
63 Lapide 1987, p.72 (Vitellius); Philo, Message to Gaius, XXXVIII (cf. wikipedia, Pilatus).
64 Lapide 1987, p.73: "by conservative estimate roughly sixthousand Jews ... "
65 Lapide 1987, p.72, referring to church historian Eusebios.

soberly states.[66] Matthew makes a casting out of it, for showmaster Pilate gives the crowd free choice: "Whom do you want me to release for you, Barabbas or Jesus who is called the Messiah?" And as Pilate's motive Matthew adds: "For he knew that for envy they had delivered him." (27:17-18). If so, shouldn't he have foreseen clearly that they would decide against this man whom he could save much easier by a simple word of command, playing the casting game instead with the two "robbers" he anyway would crucify besides the loser of the casting?

Much more informative, however, than this little Freudian slip of Matthew in his attempt to paint the Roman beautiful and the Jews ugly is the wording of the Greek original text, Here the preceding verse 16 reads: *Eichon de tóte desmion epísmenon legómenon Iesoun Barabban* – "At that time they had a notorious prisoner, called Jesus Barabbas." Now Pilate asks the Jewish people: *Tina thélete apolýso hymín: Iesoun ton Barabban e Iesoun ton legómenon christón* – "Whom do you want me to release for you, Jesus Barabbas or Jesus who is called the Messiah?"

The strange coincidence that this *Bar Abbas*, literally *Son of Father*, bore the first name *Jesus* had startled already Church Father Origen (185-254). Can a robber, he asked himself, bear such a holy name? During the following centuries, the name "Jesus Barabbas" was suppressed in most of the handwritten gospel copies. Why? Meticulously my Catholic "Jerusalem Bible" of 1968 hints in a tiny footnote concerning Mt 27:16 at the "Other reading (here and v.17): Jesus Barabbas". Yet in 1946, and by timely reasons, Jules Isaac had hinted gently to this reading: "Why should I conceal the suspicion that obtrudes on me against my will and foreshadows ... that it's been the one and real Jesus for whose pardon the Jewish crowd entreated?"[67]

How the twin question "Jesus the Barabbas or Jesus the Messiah" was born, Hyam Maccoby explains: "All gospels get embarrassed because in the earlier part of the story they have emphasized Jesus' general belovedness so much. This inevitably led to a stumbling transition when later on they wanted to underscore the whole Jewish people's guilt in the crucifixion of Jesus. In the original gospel, Jesus never at all was rejected by the Jewish people or their religious lea-ders, the Phariseans. His enemies among the Jews were the Sad-

---

66 Isaac, p.337.
67 Isaac, p.393.

duceans and the Herodians."[68] That Jesus himself belonged to the progressive, popular group of intellectuals called the Pharisees may be seen yet in his exclusively pharisean title *rabbi* which, contrary to the collaborant Sadduceans with their hereditary titles of Levites and Cohanim, signified wisdom acquired by learning.[69] At any rate, the scission between Jesus and the Pharisees was rather harmless compared to the Jekyll-Hydean scission between Jesus and Barabbas.

Within his crowd, his kin: Barabbas, painted by French artist James Tissot (1836-1902)

Purpose and construction of the dramatic element "Enter Barabbas" Maccoby explains: "When Jesus was in Pilate's prison, the crowd surrounded the building and called for his release. This was quite a natural thing for them, just continuing their fervent support for him during his triumphant entry and later on. This fact could not be suppressed completely since it based on a strong tradition, but it posed a big problem for later gospel editors who wanted to show Jesus as being rejected by the whole people. They could not deny that the Jewish people called for Jesus' release but they found a clever solution" – make two of one! "Indeed the Jewish people shouted to Pilate he should release Jesus Barabbas, but only because Jesus Barabbas was

68 Maccoby 1996, p.114.
69 Ben-Chorin 1980, p.185; Lapide (1987, p.111) counts 14 NT mentions of Jesus as rabbi.

the name of the man who was also known as Jesus of Nazareth."[70]
Changing *Jesus Barabbas* to *Jesus or Barabbas* was to Jesus' scribes
as featherlight as it was weighty for Barabbas' kin.

How came that Jesus' sympathisers in their Aramaic everyday language called him Bar Abbas? In his well-known Father-verses of **Mt 6:9/ Lk 11:2** (Our Father prayer) **Mt 7:11/ Lk 11:13** (If you give good gifts ... how much more your Father), **Mt 6:32 / Lk 12:30** (Your Father knows ...) and the already quoted **Mt 18:14** (not the will of your Father in heaven that one of these little ones ...) he never refers to *his*, but always to *your* father, stubbornly denying the Son-of-God role Paul would make out of his salient habit of relating to God as Father. "There are some examples of other rabbis in the Talmud who called God 'Abba', but Jesus maybe has made a tantamount conspicuous habit out of this that he came to be called 'Barabbas' by nickname, marking his close relationship with God."[71] Maccoby's view is plausible, but since his proofs (Mk 14:36; Mt 23:9; Rom 8:15; Gal 4:6) are scarce, the more convincing seems how Rabbi Bonder relates the name Bar Abbas to the times of Roman raids when *someone had to assume fathership for these sons who were not marginalized by any means*: "The Aramaic name Bar Abbas or bar-ha-aba literally means Son of Father ... Individuals without a confirmed father could name themselves 'Son of the father', either in the sense of a 'divine fatherhood' – or even in ironic form. This denomination, central to the messianic tensions of redemption of the fatherless sons who threaten Jewish continuity, is very significant." So Bonder, living in a land with so many *mães solteiras* (single mothers) puts the accent quite different from Maccoby when he strongly backs the British scholar's reading of Pilate's judgment, "... that there were not two to be judged but only one – Jesus, the bar ha-abba, the son of the father."[72]

The editorial cleaving between Jesus and Barabbas was not very smooth, however. The rapidness with witch the "Hosianna!" was followed by the "Crucify him!" has become proverbial (notably in German) for an abrupt ungrateful revulsion. A disloyal bunch that had welcomed him a week before as "a very large crowd" with palmtree-branches (Mt 21:8); a crowd that in the quantity of "all the people" short time later came to meet him in the temple (John 8:2); a crowd that also Luke terms "all the people", that was "spellbound

70 Maccoby 1996, p.114.
71 Maccoby 1996, p.115.
72 Bonder 1998, p.101.

by what they heard" from his lips (Luke 19:48) and later as "a large crowd of the people and of women who were mourning and lamenting" accompanied him with solidarity on his last walk (Luke 23:27) – this very bunch and what's worse, "all of them" (Mt 27:22), the "people as a whole" (Mt 27:25) in between is heard shouting for his crucifixion and his blood to come upon them.

Rather, says Maccoby, not the people as a whole but an alarming crowd had summoned in front of Pilate's palace – to call for what? The two details that this "notorious prisoner" (Mt 27:16) named Bar-Abbas "had been thrown into prison for an insurrection in the city ..." (Lk 23:19) and that the people wanted him to be released, are two well-linked puzzle parts which now fall to the right place: the place of an insurrector, well-loved by a people that in front of the Prefect's windows had chorused the name of their man of hope, preferring his nickname since it sounded much more rhythmic and aggressive: Je-shú ha Bar-Abbas, Bar-Abbas ha Bar-Abbas!

Bar Abbas, the Son Daddy's: What did this father want him to do?

Zechariah provided the man so close to God, now heading for God's holy mountain, with a rather complete program, starting with instructions for "the zenith of Jesus' political career",[73] his entrance to the city: "Shout in triumph, O daughter of Jerusalem! See, your king is coming to you ... humble, riding on an ass, on a donkey foaled by a she-ass. He shall banish chariots from Ephraim and horses from Jerusalem ..." (9:9-10). "On that day the Lord their God will rescue his people" (9:16). Superior Roman forces? No problem: "In that day, a great panic from the Lord shall fall upon them ... and everyone shall raise his hand against everyone else's hand" (14:13). Zechariah reminds him of a low point: the city captured, "the houses plundered, the women violated" but right in the next verse he tells him where the final battle would be started: "Then the Lord will come forth and make war on those nations ... he will set His feet on the Mount of Olives, near Jerusalem on the east, and the Mount of Olives shall split across from east to west ..." After the battle, "all who survive of all those nations that came up against Jerusalem shall make a pilgrimage year by year to bow low to the King Lord of Hosts" (14:2-16). In other words: The Panthera-father, tamed in due time, would bow low to the good father.

---

73 Maccoby 1996, p.91.

This conscious working toward death

Regardless of whether he intended to be the breaker through the occupier phalanx of Roman superpower or the abolisher of highly profitable Jewish temple sacrifice: Didn't he have to suppose that he himself would be his project's most predictable victim?

That Jesus' fanatism "bordered to insanity" German theologian David Friedrich Strauß had asserted yet in 1864. In 1910, Dr. Charles Binet-Sanglé published his book *La Folie de Jesus* diagnosing Jesus' illness as "religious paranoia" on grounds of seven gospel-related details which he classified as halluzinations. In 1912, prominent New York psychiatrist Dr. William Hirsh agreed with Binet-Sanglé's opinions and pointed to Jesus' "megalomania, which mounted ceaselessly and immeasurably". Hirsh concluded that "everything that we know about him conforms so perfectly to the clinical picture of paranoia that it is hardly conceivable that people can even question the accuracy of the diagnosis."[74]

In 1933, the Alsacian theologist, brillant organ player and famous "jungle doctor" Albert Schweitzer wrote in his book *Die psychiatrische Beurteilung Jesu* (The Psychiatric Diagnosis of Jesus), that "this conscious working toward his death can by no means be interpreted, as Binet-Sanglé seems to be inclined to, as a morbid self-sacrifice ...". Rather, indeed, this victimal death "represents a necessary element of Jesus' messianic thinking and acting."[75] In Schweitzer's view, Jesus wanted to take the birthpangs of messianic age on himself, believing strongly in the big bang, the final clash initiating the kingdom of God – yet before the barley harvest. "As preparation for this he sent out his disciples to warn his fellow Jews. He was convinced that his disciples were going to suffer in this task. When they returned uninjured, he was constrained to bring God, so to say, into a compulsed-move situation. Therefore he himself stepped into foreground, not only as messenger of God's kingdom, but also as God's suffering servant."[76]

In Dr. Schweitzer's view, Jesus behaved "totally different from a persecuted paranoid", since he didn't stay inactive and defensive but by provoking actions attempted "to enforce an intervention against himself". The thesis of his colleagues Binet-Sanglé and Hirsh that

---

74 Havis, Don: An Inquiry Into the Mental Health of Jesus: Was He Crazy? In: Secular Nation, 2/2001, San Mateo, CA (sfatheists.com).
75 Schweitzer, p.36-37.
76 De Rosa, p.179 and Nicholls, p.25.

Jesus suffered from a "*relationship mania* insofar as Jesus related the prophets' messianic passages to himself" Schweitzer counters similarly to Maccoby, interpreting this behaviour of Jesus "in an adequate historical consideration of his standpoint [as] a thoroughly normal psychological performance".[77]

As to the childhood trauma of Jesus ben Pantera, right here Hirsh's viewpoint might come to grip: "We have here a boy with extraordinary mental talents, who however is predisposed to psychic disturbances and who by and by develops fixed ideas. His complete leisure time he uses for the study of 'holy' texts, whose reading certainly contributed to his mental illness."[78]

Did he read the story of Jephthah, the strong warrior – and son of a harlot – who was first expulsed by his stepbrothers, then called back and put to the top of a victorious army as "their commander and chief" (Judges 11)?

Did he identify with Samson, this archetype of suicide attacker also described in the book of Judges (13-16)? Samson's story starts with the angel of Yahve announcing to a barren Danite woman: "You will conceive and bear a son ... and he will be the first to deliver Israel from the Philistines".

Whereas Samson was famous for his physical strength, the charismatic Galilean preacher Jesus (who according to Celsus, the Acts of Peter and Acts of John in 2nd as well as Ephrem Syrus in 4th century was small, according to a disputed Roman source but 150 centimeters tall)[79] was himself surprised and impressed by the healing effects of his mere presence, of his layed-on hands or the mere touching of his garment by health-seekers; that is, by "thin membrane" qualities found frequently in people with prenatal trauma.[80] Did he, who apparently could heal all illnesses, expulse all demons by imposing his hands – did he deem himself able to deliver Israel from the Roman legions just sort of imposing his hands on the Mount of Olives?

The gospel statements about his impassibility during the examination are thoroughly plausible to Maccoby, "not because of surrender to death or the wish for crucifixion but out of total despair and deception ... So much had he relied on the expected miracle on Mount of Olives that his complete apocalyptic system of redemption was

---

77 Schweitzer, p.15 and 30.
78 Schweitzer, p.22.
79 Wikipedia article "Race and appearance of Jesus"; Roman source: Lehmann, p.10-11.
80 Alberti, p.172.

broken now."[81] The father up there didn't intervene, the Roman does not yield to *vox populi*, just speaks three words to him, if any: "Ibis in crucem!" – You'll go to the cross. And thus it happened that this Bar-Abbas who one week before, celebrated by the people, had entered the city through the eastern gate riding over green branches of hope; and who had paced the eastern gate again to pray on the Mount of Promise, was to leave Jerusalem again through the northern gate with a timber on his shoulder.

The last walk of a man whom many had taken for Messiah. His last cry "Eli, Eli, lama sabachthani? – My God, my God, why have you forsaken me" (Mk 15:34) – is the first verse of Psalm 22. It matches the voluntary father-loving self-sacrifice á la Paul like a dementi – and like an exclamation mark his hope for the good father above, against the bad Roman father below.

One more failed Messiah. *Awanim u meshugaim* – "stones and loonies" are abundant in Jerusalem, a Jewish proverb rightly states until today. In 2008, the city's police central had to take care for the new record number of more than 200 male tourists who right here became convinced to be Jesus. Jerusalem lies on the hills, thousand meters above sea level, quite chilly, too much hotness may hardly be the reason. Rather too many crosses, anchored in children's souls years ago and now erupting here, where people died on them.

Last and first, the women

On his way uphill to Golgotha, "a large crowd trailed behind, including many grief-stricken women". And these women are the last human beings he speaks to: "Daughters of Jerusalem, don't weep for me, but weep for yourselves and for your children ..." (Luke 23:27-28). Women who had followed him from Galilee watched his torment "from a distance. Among them were Mary Magdalene, Mary the mother of James the younger and of Joseph, and Salome" (Mark 15:40). As "standing near the cross" John (19:25) depicts "Jesus' mother, and his mother's sister, Mary (the wife of Clopas), and Mary Magdalene". Even the drinks offered to him allegedly by the soldiers generally were a task of women: While the vinegar mentioned in all four gospels was a cheap thirst-quencher, Mark's "wine spiced with myrrh" points to a custom mentioned in the Talmud: Noble women used to ease the victims' awful fate by narcotic drinks.

---

81 Maccoby 1996, p.107.

And women were the ones who sticked by him after his failure. Matthew (27:61) mentioned "Mary of Magdala and the other Mary" taking part in his burial. Two days later, "when the Sabbath was over, Mary Magdalene, Mary the mother of James [as well as of Jesus, Joseph, Judas, Simon] and Salome bought spices, so they might go and anoint him." When they arrive at the grave, the shutter stone is rolled aside, the grave is empty, save for a young man dressed in a white robe explaining: "He has been raised. He is not here. Look, there is the place they laid him. But go, tell his disciples and Peter that he is going ahead of you to Galilee; there you will see him, just as he told you" (Mk 16:1-8).

Why do the three women who had been so close to Jesus in his lifetime now flee from the tomb, as "terror and amazement had seized them and they said nothing to anyone, for they were afraid"? And why does Mark's final chapter in his authentic form end so mundanely without any actual witness of resurrection, whereas yet some fifteen years earlier Paul had assured the Corinthians (1:15) neatly: "He was raised on the third day in accordance with the scriptures and appeared to Cephas, then to the twelve [i.e. including Judas]. Then he appeared to more than five hundred brothers at one time ... then to James, then to all the apostles. Last of all, as to one untimely born, he appeared also to me"? The explanation of the discrepancy resides within Paul's last words: Just as Jesus had "appeared also to me" more than ten years after his crucifixion, namely in a non-physical but spiritual vision, thus Paul alleges Jesus to have appeared to the leading figures of the Jerusalem community. Paul's spiritual, visionary interpretation of Christ's resurrection – note that according to Paul so far no female sinful being had seen the raised redeemer – contrasts strikingly to the sober report of the three Jewish women who never claimed to have seen the person so dear to them in his lifetime newly alive now after his death on the cross.

How did they have spent, or better say come through the Sabbath after his crucifixion and burial? Sabbath is not for sadness. How not get drowned in depression after his death? What to read in order to gain new hope? What did *he* use to read? Maybe Hosea, chapter 6? "Come, let us return to the Lord. He has torn us to pieces; now he will heal us. He has injured us; now he will bandage our wounds. In two days He will make us whole again; *on the third day* he will raise us up ... *His appearance* is as sure as *daybreak* ... for I desire goodness, not sacrifice; knowledge of God instead of sacrifice."

On the third day, at *daybreak*, his sister Salome, his mother Mary and his friend Mary from Magdala went to the tomb. *His appearance?* The tomb is empty.

Crossan disputes the empty tomb as an historical fact, but Geza Vermes argues that this emptyness is rooted too deeply in tradition to be dismissed as untrue, since within the passion narratives this empty tomb is rather "the one solid fact underlying all these stories".[82] Matthew enshrouds this *solid fact* into one more plot story including this time an angel in white clothing and Pilate's dumbstruck guards bribed by the Jews to spread the lie of the stolen corpse. Luke hasn't heard that rumour, but he has not one man but two men in white and the *solid fact* confirmed by the third man Peter who "ran to the tomb ... and looking in, he saw the linen cloths by themselves". Contrarily, John is moved by *the one solid fact* to provide, among all gospels, the historically most correct description of the "burial customs of the Jews" in a rock tomb typical of Jesus' time.

Historical fact is that these tombs were made for a two-steps-burying: The embalmed corpse remained stretched-out therein until one year later its dried bones were put into a small ossuary to remain in the tomb together with other ossuaries.

If we suppose a vanished corpse had been the starting point of all these visions (as the majority of scholars assumes), we are left with two interpretations: Either the corpse was removed or put into another tomb – what Matthew (28:11-15) disputes by means of ascribing bribery to the usual suspects. Or, the crucified one was not really actually truly dead which John (19:33-35) denies by means of physical evidence (broken legs, side wound, embalming).

Flavius Josephus, who died in 100 CE, in his biography (section 75) remembers a friend who really rose from crucifixion: "I saw many captives crucified, and remembered three of them as my former acquaintance. I was very sorry at this in my mind, and went with tears in my eyes to Titus, and told him of them; so he immediately commanded them to be taken down, and to have the greatest care taken of them, in order to their recovery; yet two of them died under the physician's hands, while the third recovered."

In Jewish jurisdiction, the fact that a man had been seen hanging on the cross was not taken for a valid proof of his death. According to the Talmud, the spouse of a crucified man could marry newly only if trustworthy witnesses had stated her husband's death or he himself

---

82 Nicholls, p.117.

from high on cross had agreed to divorce. For tradition has cases of crucified ones who hung up to five days on beams and life, persevering long enough "to obtain their pardon from the Romans by means of bribe and, taken down from cross, to be nursed to health again."[83] "Nursed to health" is a metaphor of enticing humaneness. However, neither will I indulge in speculation about a happier end of Jesus' life, nor do I subscribe to Crossan's worst case scenario in which he explains the empty tomb, as well as the fact that "of all other thousands of Jews crucified around Jerusalem in that terrible first century ... we have found only one skeleton and one nail", with "the dogs again, at worst".[84] The best case scenario probably would start with "the richest matrons among 'the dear women of Jerusalem' who, as we read, attended crucifixions and by bribing soldiers and officials sometimes achieved to have a still respiring victim taken down from the cross."[85] And best case could finish, since the ends of Mark's, Matthew's and John's gospels point to Galilee, with the "grave of Jesus tradition" to which the famous 16th century Kabbalist Isaac Luria refers and that in any case expresses high esteem: Luria says that Jesus lies buried near Galilee's mountain top city of Safed, and counts his grave among "the burial places of the righteous".[86]

End and beginning
No Christian theology explains how the phallic cross of his end is linked in the phallic violence of his inception. Correct Christmas Plays sweeten the beginning and thus exacerbate the hate against the Jews who on schedule will crucify the manger child yet shortly before Easter.
So independent of the season Miriam's Midwives bring to light quite something. First of all they give Miriam, who in Christian view unasked fell pregnant by the Lord of Universe, the honor of an innocent, traumatized by male violence yet resilient young female victim, loving her unwanted child against all odds.
This unwanted child became a man who campaigned for women and till this day is painted in androgynous softness but surrounded by twelve men. "Those who seek to rediscover Jesus the feminist over

---

83   Lapide 1984, passim; cf. Lapide 1988, p.84.
84   Crossan, p.188.
85   Cohn, Haim, p.239.
86   Tabor, p.295-300.

against Jewish life and beliefs" should not "relinquish those *Jewish foresisters* who entered into the vision and movement of Jesus", warns Catholic theologian Elisabeth Schüssler-Fiorenza.[87] At any rate these Jewish fore- and ances-sisters, female disciples and beardless friends of Bar Abbas existed in a realness that to Churchfathers probably was rather embarrassing and worth concealing.

Too bad, as due to the filters they installed we now are unable to reconstruct what these contemporaries imported into Jesus' public discourse. Herself being a present-day disciple of Jesus, Rosemary Radford Ruether deplores that the male monotheistic God amplified domination in many areas: men over women, man over animals and the rest of creation. Equally obvious is to Schüssler-Fiorenza that Christian and Jewish theology after the holocaust must refuse a patriarchal God, "and it can do so only when it mourns the loss of women's contributions and rejects their theological dehumanization." Her protest is "against the destruction of life which all too often is legitimated by an abusing God who is a projection and defender of patriarchal interests."[88]

An abusing God? If in *Miriam's Midwives* the Lord of the Universe has to defend Himself before a court, this may appear as unrespectful to kyriarchal Christians, whereas Rabbi Irving Greenberg stresses that "no trial in Jewish liturgy can be authentic without including the trial of God as well."[89] Eli Wiesel's *The Trial of God (as it was held on February 25, 1649, in Shamgorod)* reenacts such a trial. But also the autobiographical "No!" of Auschwitz survivor Imre Kertész in his *Kaddish For an Unborn Child* brings the creator to court:

"No! Never could I be father, fate, God of another human being, No! Never shall another child live through what I had to live through, No! it raged and roared inside me, it must not be that this childhood occurs to him – to you – to me ..."[90]

Martin Buber, by contrast, defends a humane God, charges a different one: "If the God of love and mercy, just out of his compassion, could not stand seeing that Abraham wanted to slaughter his son – how could he have permitted that his own son was killed away, and at that in the most cruel, most inhumane way on earth?"[91]

---

87 Ellis 1997, p.139.
88 Ellis,1997, p.138-139.
89 Greenberg 1993, p.213.
90 Kertesz, p.118.
91 Buber, Martin (Hg): Aggadat Bereschit. Wilna 1925, p.31 (nach Lapide 1988, p.58 f.)

And Sarah, who had named her son *itzchak*, He-will-laugh? What did she say about her son's barely forestalled patriarchal sacrifice? Nothing at all. After just five subsequent verses (Gen 22:20-24) relating proudly about the 12 sons of her sisters-in-law Milka and Reuma but not one word about Sarah, she simply dies and gets buried in Hebron. Epitaph by humanistic rabbi Edward Klein: "Sarah leaves Abraham, never to rejoin him or speak another word to him until her death, which may well have been caused by what happened to Isaac."[92]

At any rate, the valid version of the story has Isaac's sacrifice cancelled by God, to put an end to any human sacrifice.

The victim son of Miriam became a prominent opponent of violence. Such a praise of Jesus appears naive and mealy-mouthed in view of the innumerable violent words of Jesus delivered in the gospels. By good reasons however, German New Testament scholar Gerd Lüdemann regards none of the threatfully violent words of Jesus concerning the Christian hell complex (Mt 5:22, 8:12, 10:15, 10:28, 11:22-24, 18:7-9, 22:13 ...) as authentic – including the verse Mt 25:41, painted by Michelangelo onto the wall of Sixtine Chapel and slightly reminding on selection in Auschwitz: When the Son of Man comes in his glory, "he will say to those on his left: Depart from me, you who are cursed, into the eternal fire ...". Such praise of fire would be more than strange for a Jesus whose truest followers, the Ebionites, wanted to extinguish the fire of animal sacrifice in the temple. "Ebionites" was the later name of the Nazoreans or Nazarenes (Acts 24:5) who themselves were the successors of the early Church of Jerusalem; Jesus himself is called a Nazarenos (Mk 14:67) as well as Nazoraios (Acts 4:10). The vegetarian Ebionites viewed Jesus as a purely human prophet like Moses, as a reformer of Jewish law. They believed in resurrection of the dead and hoped for the return of Jesus; they practiced non-violence including refusal of military service. True to their master they rejected burnt offerings, substituting their flames by an extinguishing element: the waters of baptism. And clear as water was their reason why they had to reject Paul's doctrine of redemption by Jesus' bloody sin offering: In their view, "Jesus had established baptism as a means of purification and atonement in the place of the bloody animal sacrifices. In so doing he merely ac-

---

92   Edward J.Klein, "My Jewish Odyssey", in: Humanistic Judaism, No.1, 2105, Farmington Hills, Michigan, p.40-41. Klein differs from R.E.Friedman (p.330, 331, 345) in ascribing Gen 22:11-16a not to P, but to the Yahvist J-source.

complished what yet Moses had desired: the abolition of the animal sacrifices. [...] Christianity had been freed from the Jewish sacrificial worship not through the universally efficacious sacrifice of the son, as the Church which followed Paul believed, but rather through the water of baptism whereby Jesus had extinguished the fire of the sacrificial cult."[93]

Jesus, who called a little child to him, placed the child among them and said: "Truly I tell you, unless you change and become like little children, you will never enter the kingdom of heaven" – this Jesus took a stand for the three groups most strongly threatened by male violence: children, women, animals. And he got misused to justify a celibate which seems to have contributed to not a minor extent to priestly abuse of children. The cross onto which he has been carved as Lamb of God for thousand years has justified violence against animals for thousand years, it heralds a contempt of the body which ran into contempt, if not into the burning, of women, and as black cross of crusades it was and is displayed on tanks, warships, warplanes with which German armies in two world wars destroyed Europe and six million descendants of Jesus' alleged crucifiers.

In his essay *Man into Wolf* the Jewish philosopher Robert Eisler describes how the raping of women is connected with the transition of our early human ancestors to meat consumption. At the animal we learn to be violent. Propensity towards violence was rewarded by survival, became a genetical advantage for the offspring of men who learned to skip over instinctive restrictions against sadistic impulses: These new (genetical and social) tribes "preyed on the more conservative fruit-gathering human herds reluctant to adopt the bloodthirsty new mode of life, killing the males, raping and enslaving the females, falling upon them ... "[94] Some hundreds of millennia later, German Black Forest born Gabriele Schwab, now a professor of literature in California, writes in "Haunting Legacies": "There are forms of violence – the *Holocaust, genocide, torture* and *rape* – that are considered beyond representation. Yet they also call for speech, testimony, and witnessing". Miriam and the Midwives evidence that even the outrageous kind of violence they suffered is not "beyond representation" but instead calls for coming to speech and onto stage. "We need", writes Schwab, "a theory of traumatic

---

93 Schoeps, Hans-Joachim, p.60 and 83.
94 Eisler, p.37.

narrative that deals with the paradox of telling what cannot be told or what has been silenced."[95]

And the extreme torture of crucifixion which is not beyond representation? Doesn't it resemble rape as "regress to a catastrophic helplessness akin to that of an abused child"?[96] The cross, as the graphically formed torture closely linked with the genocides that started in 1492 and 1942, marked the end of a life whose outset in sexual violence could not be told or has been silenced. Miriam's Midwives play and narrate it.

"Theater is about embodying emotions, giving voice to them, becoming rhythmically engaged, taking on and embodying different roles." American psychiatrist Bessel van der Kolk, born 1943 in occupied Holland, in this sense views theater as physical therapy, too: "Theater is about finding ways of telling the truth and conveying deep truths to your audience."[97] In the way of *Boston Trauma Drama* described by Van der Kolk, in the sense of Augusto Boal's *Teatro dos Oprimidos* as well as Jacob Levy Morenos Psychodrama, Miriam's Midwives could have releasing effects for an ensemble of women traumatized by violence.

Let's end with an utopian verse well known to Miriam's son: "The wolf will live with the lamb, the leopard will lie down with the goat, the calf and the lion and the yearling together; and a little child will lead them" (Isaiah 11:6). Today, or for quite some time, it's time for reverting the predatorization – *Man Into Wolf* – of our species. time for a silver lining Robert Eisler spots on the horizon:

"As Carl Jung saw so clearly, the tradition of a 'Fall from the Garden of Eden' is an archetype ... If, however, there was a most definite Fall, if 'human nature' was originally not lupine but that of a peaceful, frugivorous, non-fighting and not even jealous animal, which developed its present predatory, murderous and jealous habits only under extreme environmental pressure by extra-specific imitation of the blood-lustful enemies of its own species, then there is hope of changing our social organization and our environment, gradually or suddenly, in such a way that we can throw the fatal wolf's mask,

---

95 Schwab, p.48: „There are forms of violence – the *Holocaust, genocide, torture* and *rape* – that are considered beyond representation. Yet they also call for speech, testimony, and witnessing".
96 Schwab, p.153.
97 Van der Kolk, p.337.

tame the 'archetypal' beast in ourselves, and restore mankind to its pristine state of *ahimsa* or in-nocence, so achieving peace on earth for men of good will."[98]

During the last world war, brought over Poland by a sensitive Austrian boy almost beaten to death by his father, a son who used to educate his German Shepherd Dog in the same way and wanted to be called "Herr Wolf" himself, Itzig Manger wrote the following song whose melody Miriam's Midwives sing:

Unter di khurves fun poyln	Under the ruins of Poland
a kop mit blonde hor.	a head, blond hair, is it you?
Der kop un zay der khurbn,	The head and also the ruins
beyde zenen vor.	both are equally true.
Iber di khurves fun poyln	Onto the ruins of Poland
falt un falt a shney.	fall tender flakes, it is snow.
Der blonder kop fun mayn meydl	The curly locks of my girlfriend
tut mir mezukn vey.	take and shake me with woe.
Dolye mayn dolye, dolye, dolye mayne.	Fortune, my bad fortune ...

Der veytik zitst baym shraybtish	At the desk sits my heartsore
un shraybt a langen briv.	a letter flows from its pen.
Di trer in zayne oygn	The tear that falls from its lashes,
iz emezdik un tif.	springs from a deep den.
Iber di khurves fun poyln	Over the ruins of Poland
flatert a foygl um.	flutters trembling a bird.
A groyzer shive foygl,	The big bird's song is of mourning,
er tsitert mit di fligl frum.	a pious song never heard.
Dolye mayn dolye, dolye, dolye mayne.	Fortune, my bad fortune ...

Der groyze shive foygl,	The big bird's song, it is tearing,
mayn dershlogn gemit:	my spirit shattered in gloom:
Er trogt oyf zayne fligl	Right on his wings he is bearing
dos dozike troyer lid	this gruesome dolorous tune.
Dolye mayn dolye, dolye, dolye mayne.	Fortune, my bad fortune ...

---

98 Eisler, p.44 and 51-52..

B   On Stage

MIRIAM'S MIDWIVES
Four Women Play Nativity

Persons:
Miriam, an unwed young woman big with child receives the visit of three friends, namely:
Abigal
Michal
Dinah

Time: 3 BC   **Place**: Nazareth in Galilee

Props: Cooking pots serving as helmets and drums
A wooden bench without rest
A distaff with loose wool
A spindle with whorl (see below)
A broom
A hammer.

Spindles, with whorls made of chamotte (left: Viking, 6th century) respectively of lard stone and clay.

1. Scene: The three midwives on their way to Miriam

Overturap – thus could be called the play's musical overture, performed by the midwives.

Dinah, a more seasoned woman, wearing a cloth bag on her shoulder, enters from the left and walks to center stage, turns and continues "walking" (on the spot) towards the audience.

Dinah: When they're coming
pretty woman take a bath in manure
when they're coming,
village beauty you're too pooty
run away or be their booty
when they're coming
quickly make yourself pug-ugly
and maybe you will be lucky
when they're coming,
southern belle you will do well
with smell like hell that's what I tell you
when they're coming,
Or rather let them take their fodder,
snuff from their mouths the guys' malodor
when they're coming.
No offence, just pickin' chicken,
first the huggin' then the fuckin'
when they're coming,
No offence, don't lose your sense
you got the pussy, we the pens.

(Abigal, also with cloth bag, has entered from the right and now stands waiting undecided nearby Dinah).

Dinah: Come on now.

(Both go on walking on the spot, speaking the Rap now together. Abigal takes a metal pot from her bag and beats the rhythm with a spoon).

Both: Little girl, you should have patience
with the rapers of all nations
needing vags for their libations
when they're coming.

Just beware of men on mission,
with or lacking circumcision,
men of any land and region,
eminently Roman legion
when they're coming.

Hear my warning, you beginners,
it's the natural right of winners.
They need vags to drain their sacks,
attractive teenies for their penis.
It is all about erection,
power, nailing, satisfaction
when they're coming

Listen baby, real man
is a thing that must and can.
Just know that any man who's living
cannot keep himself from giving:
That's why you should not be shunning
when they're coming.

Know that no one stops the drive
and drive rhymes perfectly with wife
and if the outcome is new life – come on!
I tell you baby with no shamming
to manly force there is no damming
when you hear the legion drumming,
when they're coming.
.

(Michal, likewise laden, has come from the left, is looking quizzical-
ly at Dinah and Abigal).

Abigal: Come on now!

(They walk on with their Rap, now accompanied also by Michal's rhythm instrument, a vessel with dry grains).

Threesome: Little lady, you should praise
God in heaven for his ways,
as thanks to them it has come true
and ultimately you are too
Expecting.
And when the baby, little lady
if God allows opens your mouth
and you will lift him to your chest
and he will suck from both your breasts
he drinks it all and you recall:
this child is whose?

It's from one who gratis screws
the little ladies of the Jews,
it's from one whose gorgeous member
you from now on will remember
fettered to it now forever,
this fatal day will leave you never
date of shame, of eating game
the day they came.

Abigal: On a nice sunny morning like this one.

Michal: It's gonna be a hot day today, my mother said.

Abigal: Today?

Michal: No, that day, back then.
By the way, Dinah.

Dinah: Hm?

Michal: I think it proper.

Dinah: What?

Michal: Your idea that we should visit Miriam.

Dinah: There should we three meet again.

Michal: But do your really think it will help her?

Dinah: Why not?

Michal: Reopen the old sore?

Abigal: Three old sores. Your sore, Michal, my sore, and the sore of Miriam, soon to burst open now. Dinah, you as the most seasoned midwife of Nazareth, how did you hit on this idea? Why do you make us three virgins meet again?

Dinah: Why?

Michal: Yes, why?

Dinah: Abigal, you didn't get pregnant. Michal, you didn't stay pregnant. But Miriam?

Michal: So you think Miriam has the hardest time while we two dodged it, have scraped past it, got off cheaply? Do you think I ever will be able to forget how the three legionaries stood around me?

Abigal: To forget how this pig has thrown me on the ground, you think this will get out again some day, out of my head, out of my body?

Michal: Forget how the three dirty pigs have asked me, nu, did you like getting swept through properly once again?

Abigal: Nu, baby, won't you bow your thanks to me? Didn't I give it to you and duly terrific?

Michal: Sure she did enjoy it, or why would she have puffed so loudly and shaken her behind? A legionaire's ever prepared.

Abigal: Titus knows what girls desire.

Michal: Please, Abigal, don't say that once again. You know it is exactly what he said.

Abigal: What? Titus knows what girls desire?)

(Beside herself, Michal throws Abigal to the ground).

Michal: I told you don't you say that once again. I just can't stand that, it's all coming over me again just like back then. Just as I now lie above you, he back then has lied above me puffing and blowing his malodor in my face and stomping his penis inside me below. Yes, this way, again and again, and his comrades laughed and said (she speaks and acts with her lower body in coital rhythm): Tougher, man, yeah tougher, give her what she deserves, give it alright so she will know how Romans use to go in, come on buddy, don't be lame and don't you shame the army and the name of Ro-o-o-ome! (Exhausted and distraught, she lets her head sink down alongside Abigal's head, but quickly comes to again).
Excuse me, Abigal. I beg your pardon. It suddenly burst out of me.

Abigal: No problem, I understand entirely. I'm very understanding, really. And who should understand you if not I? But please, please don't you do that once again, okay?

Michal: Dinah, did you see that? You saw it and you know how all this sticks inside us to this day. So how should we two achieve to help our Miriam?

Dinah: Who else? Who else could help her if not you two, we three?

Abigal: Fair enough then. We three will meet again.

(They sing to the melody of „Unter di khurves fun poyln")

Dinah: To the house of our Miriam
Leads us the morning star.
Come on, you mourning Miriam,
and overcome your jar.

All: Miriam, little Miriam,

Miriam, little Miriam,
Miriam, little Miriam,
Miriam, little Miriam.

Abigal: Over the house of our Miriam
Nine times grinned yet the moon,
So fat and far and so careless
So cold and out of tune.

All: Miriam, little Miriam,
Miriam, little Miriam,
Miriam, little Miriam,
Miriam, little Miriam.

Michal: Smash those Romannish faces
With heavy maces of stone.
Then we will gladly forgive them
and graciously condone.[99]

All: Miriam, little Miriam,
Miriam, little Miriam,
Miriam, little Miriam,
Miriam, little Miriam.

Dinah: No. Forgetting won't help, forgiving won't either. Miriam
is young, needs strengths for a life, no, two lives.
I want her to get over it. I want a faint smile to rise on her face and a
silent yes to caress her belly.
If I succeed in bringing just a little smile onto Miriam's face. Only a
gentle No-but-Yes. That's what would make me glad.

---

99 Note: These four unwomanly brutal lines reverberate almost literally the final
words of the infamous arsonist, murderer of Jenny Towler and Shmul Meier and
raper of a minor widow, concluding the *Ballade of Macheath Begging Forgiveness*
in Bertolt Brecht's *Threepenny Opera*.

2nd Scene: In Miriam's house, in Miriam's body

Dinah: Miriam? Where are you?

Abigal: Maybe she already walked out to work on the fields?

Michal: Und where's her family? Maybe we should just go home again simply.

Dinah: I've promised her, and she promised me that she would be at home. Probably the family is out on the fields and Miriam's just a moment gone to privy. With nine month, the baby presses on the bladder. (She sits down on the floor)

Abigal: Und what is the baby in her belly thinking, in the little head that presses on her bladder? I think I can imagine.

Michal: You think you can?

Abigal: Please help me, Michal, I want to be the child now in Miriam's belly.
(Her back head-down supported by Michal, placing her head in Dinah's lap, Abigal speaks ...) Mame, do you hear me? I know it's not your fault that I am here inside you. But what will be when I come out? Will they call me Roman bastard? Will they give me a funny nickname like little Romulus? Or Gaius, Julius, Augustus? Gaius, come her, play hide and seek with us, and hide like your daddy! Julius piss off, you smell too Roman! Augustus get lost, play with the sissies! Romulus, sit on the bench, you son of a wench.

Michal: Abigal, you're vicious.

Abigal: I'm not vicious, children are vicious. And I can easily imagine ...

Michal: ... what the kids next door will say? You're sure? Doesn't it depend on what those children hear from their parents?
(Miriam enters, hardly visible, in the background).

Abigal: And what is it that they hear from them?

Michal: Maybe that Miriam's son is Jewish like any other Jew because Miriam is as innocent as all the Jewish girls the Romans like to nail down by penis while the boys get nailed up on crosses?

Abigal: Michal, you're naive. You don't want to see how much human beings like to exclude, to shove away and laugh at other human beings.

Michal: That's just one side. Think back on our childhood. You remember Malka?

Abigal: The daughter of Jokebed?

Michal: No one knew her father, but no one laughed at her either.

Abigal: And why not? Cause she was pretty, strong and perky and cause she used to smack even fat Joakim (she slaps her own left fist) if necessary.

Michal: And why should Miriam's son or daughter not be just as strong? Why do you write this Mene Tekel on the wall, phantasizing of malicious next door kids? Let me do it.
(Now she, like Abigal before but coming from the left puts her head in Dinah's lap) Mama, do you hear me? Don't be afraid, I won't put you to shame.

(Unnoticed, Miriam has come forth from the background).

Miriam: Who shall put whom to shame?

Abigal: Miriam, for a visit we have come. (She is the first one to hug Miriam).

Michal: Nu, everything all right, Miriam? You're looking good!

Dinah: How are you now that your baby is soon to come?

Miriam: And whom shall this baby put to shame? Folks, I have seen what you have played: You played what crosses the mind of the baby in my belly. Do you think I never put this question to myself? How often have I mused about it! How many times I pondered just about that inside my head and under my headscarf!

Dinah: And? What do you think the baby in your belly thinks?

Miriam: Sit down again, Dinah, and I will play the baby in my belly, with all that I think my son is thinking.

Michal: Your son?

Miriam: My little boy-child, right.
(She sits down, back to the audience, between Dinah's legs, then slowly lies her body on the floor and her legs on Dinah's shoulders, in order to speak now as her child head-down up to Dinah) Mame, how did I come here? And how inside of you? And why just into *you*? Of course I noticed that you did not invite me to come into your house. But now I am in here. And who has sent me to you? Who, yes, who? And didn't he know that you don't want me at all? And why, oh Mame, why don't you want me? I am your child after all, ain't I? Is it my fault that I'm inside you now? Where, then, could I have gone? Where to? Will you keep me? I promise you, I won't put you to shame.
I will always be as good as gold, will never harm a sparrow, never scare a pigeon, will always scrape my plate at dinner and always study hard at school and very diligent. Maybe I even will become a rabbi. A bookish scholarly rabbi. Look there, the son of Miriam, people will say, that's the Rabbi Bar Miriam they will say. And I promise you, if you accept me I will not bring shame on you.
(She straightens herself abrupt, turns, speaks to the audience:) I will accept you, my son, and you will be my son and you will learn the books and study hard and you will be a rabbi. A rabbi who acts justly and who cares for women and children and their rights. And you will stand on the mountain with arms spread wide and you will tell the people what is right and you'll herald liberation and put an end to all violence and you will (she starts screaming) drive out the men of violence and all the whoresons will run down the hill like a herd of two thousand pigs and drown int the see and puff no more and nevermore they will return to where they crept out of their mothers' bellies!!!

70

(She calms down again, feels her belly with both hands).
Yes, my little darling, I will take you and accept you, I promise, your mother will love you, cause it is not your fault.

3rd Scene: Why didn't you abort?

Michal: Why do you all look at me?

Dinah: We do not look at you, Michal.

Abigal: Michal, I just was lucky enough to not get pregnant.

Michal: The good luck not to get pregnant. What a fortune. What an undeserved amazing grace of God.
But me this God has planned to gift with grace and child, and he has sent to me an angel, an archangel with helmet and leathern armour to deliver his child to me. And I, ungrateful as I am, did not accept this child of God but did away with him.

Dinah: And I have helped you, Michal. And both we know why you did not want to have it and could not have it.

Michal: Why I could not have it? Because I pondered: Would the apple fall far from the tree? If this baby will be a boy, what a little man is it that I will nurse on my breasts? A Romulus with a wolf-like throat, with wolf-like teeth and wolf-like eyes who jolly wags his wolf's tail? A diligent young raper? A dashing humilizer? A gifted violator named Titus ben Michal?
And if I would give birth to this child, who else than just my rapist would I do a nice favor in the first place? Who else than those males who love and practice violence? What else would I support than the fucktual convenience of oppressing women?
And one more detail, girls: My grandma used to say: To bear a child is just as painful as to shit a claybrick. That's women's fate, she said, and men don't have to pass through that, selah. But my delivery would be much more sore. A claybrick? No, a sharp-edged rock

would I've been bound to shit if I had brought to this world's light what once this Roman bowman has shot into my belly. A raper I would rear! Why do you stare at me, the guilty one, the evil mother, the murderess of her child?

Dinah: No one stares at you, Michal ...

Michal: Just stare at Miriam. She will enrich this world with one more Roman son, with one more nail in the cross we all are hanging on.
Just do ask Miriam why she's doing this to us.

Miriam: I tell you why. I felt like you, Michal. And then I went to visit Elisabeth.

Dinah: Your cousin?

Miriam: And she read to me from the First Book of Kings. You all know the passage: Later two prostitutes came to King Solomon and stood before him ...

Abigal: Miriam, we know this story ... [1 Kings 3:16-27]

Miriam: The first woman said: Please, my lord! This woman and I live in the same house; and I gave birth to a child while she was in the house. On the third day after I was delivered, this woman also gave birth to a child. We were alone, she and me, with our babies. And in the night her baby died, because she lay on it. She arose in the night and took my son from my side while I was asleep, and laid him in her bosom; and she laid her dead son in my bosom. When I arose in the morning to nurse my son, there he was, dead. But when I looked at him closely in the morning, it was not the son I had borne.
(She turns to Dinah who now – as Solomon – sits in the middle, facing the audience)

Michal: And the other prostitute said ... (She rises): No, the live one is my son, and the dead one is yours!

Miriam: But the first insisted: No, the dead boy is yours; mine is the living one! And they went on arguing before the king (She places

72

herself, facing Solomon, opposite Michal).

Dinah: And King Solomon spoke up: One says ...

Michal: This is my son, the live one, and the dead one is yours.

Dinah: And the other says ...

Miriam No, the dead boy is yours, mine is the live one.

Dinah: So fetch me a sword.

Abigal: And a sword was brought before the king.
(She hands Dinah a long ladle and perches – as the child – between Michal and Miriam who keep facing Dinah).

Dinah: And the King said: Cut the live child in two, and give half to one and half to the other!

Miriam: No, no, my lord, give her the child, please just don't kill him!

Michal: It shall be neither yours nor mine; cut it in two!

Dinah: And Solomo spoke up: Give the live child to this woman. She is his mother.

Michal: And I am the cruel one, because I layed on my child, I layed on it my grave anguish and my heavy insensitive body. Or am I cruel because I so light-minded, so giddily chose to abort it? A child who forever would have reminded me on the brute, and forever would have bound me to the scumbag?

Dinah: The problem, no: *Your* problem is, that this baby was not just the scumbag's baby but also yours.

Michal: My own flesh and blood, affirmative! I've had to do away with part of me, just like a bitch-fox bites her own leg off when this leg holds her tight in a snap trap. (She seems to withdraw to the background ashamed, but she prepares her kind of play). A trap of iron, with snapping teeth. Iron like these cooking pots. Cooking pots? No,

that's Roman helmets. Put them on and stand around me like back then. And you, Dinah, will play the rapists, so you'll see what is my problem really. And I, I won't resist against you three.
(Abigal, Miriam and Dinah put on the pots which also cover her eyes. Dinah seizes Michal and throws her on the floor).

Dinah: How do you want us to handle you, little Jewess Michal? You may utter all your desires, your wishes are our orders and we'll read everything in your eyes.

Abigal: Don't worry, we won't harm you, quite the contrary.

Dinah: We don't want to hurt you, quite the opposite. Only if you resist the Roman army, things might get somehow unpleasant. (She kneels with spread legs above Michal and presses her shoulders to the ground). Look into my eyes, little Jewess ...

Michal: The little Jewess spits in your face!

(Abigal and Dinah pull Michal around brusque, so that she lies face-down).

Dinah: Now I will spit you something, you village bitch!

Abigal: Give her what for, comrade, and show her how it is done among the army. But don't you hurt her, right, my turn is after you!

Miriam: Let her go, you scumbags, let her go!
(She holds a spindle with yarn against Abigal).

Abigal: Boy what kind of man are you? So gay and fruity, right?

Miriam: Let her go, or ...

Abigal: Or what?

Miriam: Or I'll kill you, you pigs!

(Miriam draws the yarn from the spindle, a shining knife appears. Abigal jerks back, Dinah lets go of Michal and jumps up).

4.Szene: Miriam prophesies

Dinah: Miriam, little Miriam. Calm down. I am your friend Dinah, and it's all been just play, just play.

Abigal: Real is but the knife, right? A knife in a yarnwinder. Where did you get that, Miriam?

Michal: Miriam, it's all right, I'm okay, 't was just a play. Please give me the knife.

(Hesitantly and trembling, Miriam takes the spindle at its blade and hands it over to Michal).

Michal: Sharp like a dagger. Whence ...

Miriam: Home made.

Michal: When?

Miriam: Eight months ago. When I didn't know yet that I'm pregnant, I burned the wooden haft from an old kitchen knife and put a whorl on it.

Abigal: What for? (She looks at the spindle Michal has given her, then passes it to Dinah.)

Miriam: You ask what for?

Dinah: Miriam, now you suddenly forgot your part ...

Miriam: Forgot my part?

Dinah: But it's good that you did. Very good indeed.

Miriam: No, it isn't good. This stab in me will never heal. My raging anger against those guys will never calm. And you know why? Because they're that cowards. They feel as strong men and are the most coward pigs among all those who piss on walls [I Samuel 25:22;

I Kings 16:11]. If three lions would have mauled me, three bears had eaten me, all right. But it's been three pigs, three grinning grunting pigs on scene watching the chief pig in the leopard's skin just eating me. The father of my son is a pig, a pathetically coward pig, you understand? Tell me how to love a child whose father ...

Michal: ... whose father is not human, right?

Miriam: I have a dream almost every night. In this dream I am in the hands of three soldiers and they can treat me as they like to. Every night. When will that stop?

Dinah: It will stop – maybe – if you live it through once more, but not as a victim. That's why you built the knife into the spindle. You have to pass through that once more and come out different. If not in your dream, then here in your kitchen. Take the spindle, please, Miriam.
(Miriam takes the tool like in trance).
We can play that, don't we? With knife. Maybe this will help you, Miriam. So once again, now the other way round, suddenly three women against one man: Michal lays on on the floor, I am the pig, Miriam has the knife and Abigal this cord ... (she takes down her headscarf) to fetter me. Hands on back. And not too tight, it's just a play. Let's start again from "Now I will spit you something, you village bitch!"

(Same positions as before at that point. Abruptly, Miriam from behind of Dinah puts the knife on her throat. Dinah lets go of Michal who rolls aside. Miriam presses Dinah to the floor face downward, Abigal fetters her hands behinds her back, then they put Dinah sitting, eyes on the audience, the knife still at her throat).

Abigal: Now it's your turn. We just won't eat you, pig!

Dinah: No! No! Please not! Please let me live, I beg you! I didn't want to deal ill with you, I just wanted to have a little fun ...

Abigal: A little fun? Small portion of sex with women who don't want no sex, and much less with a filthy Roman jerk like you?

76

Dinah: Girls, that's how the game is played around the world: The women of the losers are the fun of the winners, right?

Michal: That's your rule of your game. But now we are the winners. Listen, girls, who wants to have fun with him? Miriam? Abigal? I don't either. Well, if you were a man ...

Abigal: Say that you're a pig!

Dinah: I am a pig.

Abigal: Now say: Please, girls, be judicious ...

Dinah: Please, please, girls, be judicious.

Abigal: But that's just what we're doing, boy: We are knife-sharply judicious. Swear that nevermore in your life you will defile a woman.

Dinah: I swear, nevermore.

Abigal: How can we believe you if we don't transform you into a girl before? You like girls, don't you?

Dinah: Yes I like girls.

(Miriam takes the knife from Dinah's throat, hands is over tho Michal and pensatively goes out of the scene).

Michal: Miriam, what's the matter with you?

Dinah: Are we playing it wrong? Is it not helpful this way?

Miriam: I'm not sure. Dinah is not Panthera. What you are playing is not serious. Not like back then. It's not back then. Not the smell of sweat and leather, not the sword in his hand, not his skin on mine. And revenge won't help me, because it does not help him (she fingers her womb)

Dinah: Nevertheless, just try it, please.

Miriam: Hand me the knife, Michal. Don't be afraid, Dinah. (She puts the knife on Dinah's throat as before) What's your name, pig?

Dinah: Panthera. I'm the Signifer of my company. I bear a leopard's skin, earn double pay. But please don't do me any mischief, please.

Miriam: What kind of mischief could I do you, big panther?

Dinah: You have a knife ...

Miriam: You had a penis. Remember how you stabbed me?

Dinah: But I let you live.

Miriam: Did you? Yes, you let me live with you, and lifelong. (She grasps the knife at its point and holds it vertical, the haft upward reminding of a cross) You see this knife, Roman?

Dinah: I see it. You can kill me. But please don't. I have a wife and a child.

Miriam: You have a child?

Dinah: I have a son, three months old.

Miriam: And a wife? One like you, a pig like you has son and wife?

Dinah: My son's name is Dan and my wife's is Leila, we're from Lebanon.

Miriam: Dan and Leila, how nice!

Dinah: To be exact, we're not married already, I'm just her fiancé. But during my next vacation, we ...

Miriam: Her fiancé? One like you is the betrothed of a woman?

Dinah: Leila is about your age ...

78

Miriam: My betrothed ... my fiancé Joseph has promised me he will take the child as son, as his son.
(She lowers the dagger). Let go of him.

Michal: What's on with you, Miriam? No more hate, all of a sudden? Forgiven and forgotten all at once?

Miriam: Joseph says he'll raise him and make a rebel out of him.

Michal: A rebel? Like the two thousand Varus has crucified? Miriam, come to yourself! Girl, you know what the Romans aim at when they crucify thousands of our young men and occupy thousands of our girls' bellies.

Abigal: Weed out Jews and prick in Romans, that's what they intend, to make us Romans yet in woman's womb.

Miriam: And you think you're helping me when you repeat this ten times and more? Can you turn back time nine months? I want to look ahead because ahead is my belly and ahead is life. Now listen how I scream ahead:
Yes I will name him Yehoshua, and he will not be a Roman. And he will throw them out, and he will stand on the mount of olives and draw the sword and the Lord of Hosts himself will lead the battle, and the mount of olives will split and fire will fall down from heaven and the sun will darken and in the darkness the Romans will fight one another.
And then my son will enter Jerusalem. And the broken stone out of the broken woman will become the cornerstone for Israel ... Hosianna! Praised be the one who comes out of my womb. Spread your clothes before him and branches of the palm tree when he marches in to Jerusalem!
(She sits on the bench, looking forward to the audience).

Michal: Marches in? No, off they'll take his clothes to scourge him (she rises), onto the cross they'll nail him, short shrift the Romans will give him and no God will come to his relief. Where was God nine months ago? Where was God when Varus teared out two thousand faithful from their houses and when the Romans ripped their clothes from their bodies (she tears her outer garment from her body).

79

Abigal: And when they drove them with scourges through the town and whipped the skin from their bodies until the blood streamed from their sandals (she pours red vinegar over Dinah's upper body) ...

Michal: ... and nailed their hands to beams (she spreads her arms) and drove them up the hill (she stands behind sitting Miriam), each one with a beam on his red shoulders (she grasps Miriam's arms from behind and spreads them horizontally like their own) ...
And where was God when they pulled up the beams and put them on the upright timber and nailed their feet onto as well ...
(She slowly pulls Miriam up, snuggling her head almost tenderly up to Miriam's) ... so that the sons of Israel hanging now on their nails could overlook the hills while down in the valley legionaries nailed their wives and daughters?

Dinah: You ask where God was? You nice little Jewesses ask where God was? I'll tell you: He was with the nailers! Yes, I was with the nailers! May I introduce myself? My name is Jupiter. If you would have a little bit of higher education, you Jewish country girls, then you would know that I, God Jupiter, use to use various guises to take earthly women forcibly: Europa I have taken in the guise of a bull, Antiope I took as a Satyr, Leda I screwed in the feathers of a swan and not too rarely by my acts of love with not too willing women I sired good-looking Godsons.

Abigal: (breaking loose with Miriam from the cross position) Dinah, now I must forget my part. Leave the wanton Roman god out of the play, he's not our god, is he?

Dinah: But it's our wombs that the Romans occupy, along the lines of their lustful chief godhead Jupiter. As the tree, so the fruit, like master like man.

Michal: And where is our master, our Hashem who ought to protect us and punish our enemies with strong hand?

Dinah: Yes, where is Adonai? Where is the Lord of Hosts?

Miriam: Where has he been? (She feels her belly). My God, my god, why have you forsaken us?

Michal: (screams) My God? No god! That's how we're mistaken, girls! And you can implore him on your knees, you can beg him and beseech him, Adonai Eloheinu, melech haolam, the Lord will not show up. To Moses, right, to Moses he has shown himself, at least his backside, back then when the Lord our God has made this covenant with his chosen people on Mount Sinai. A somewhat lopsided co-venant. For punishable is but one side.

Dinah: Punishable are but his servants and maidservants, not the Lord, oh no, where would we be? The Lord can do just what he likes to, he can flout the covenant, can look on how his creatures get heckled and tackled and racked and sacked. Since the Lord is also the judge, the human servant is always culprit. That's how it has always been and that's how it is until today. But here and today we'll turn the playboard and God is placed where he belongs: right in the dock ...

Michal: And who plays God?

5th Scene: God at Trial

> Judge: Dinah
> Attorney: Abigal
> Defending lawyer: Miriam
> God: Michal

Abigal: (knocks with a tin mug on the bench) Coming up before the court is the action of expectant mother Miriam, textile worker, unwed, resident in Nazareth, against God, Lord and creator of the universe, sex and residence unknown. I don't mention these facts for fun. In order not to let this trial become a farce, we should be clear in our minds that God is known to us but in those images we make of God. When we try God here we are trying just ourselves and our home-made, ever wrong and dangerous images of God. Whether I personally believe in you (she points to Michal with a giving hand) is not at issue. If you excuse my candor.

Michal: You are welcome.

Abigal: This said, I directly proceed in medias res. To begin with, the formalities. You are Yahve Elohim, creator of the universe, the God of Abraham, Isaac and Jacob.

Michal: (fastening on her ears a necklace passing below her nose, and putting onto it, forming a beard, wool from Miriams distaff) Yes Sir.

Abigal: Why do you put on this ridiculous beard?

Michal: Because, as you just said yourself, it is on images that we are passing judgement here. And though we are strictly forbidden to make images of God, he always comes as man. By good reasons: Would Abraham, Isaac and Jacob have heeded a Lady? Would thousands of bearded priests and levites serve a goddess?

Dinah: Not to mention the bearded godheads of our occupiers ...

Michal: I want to play the God the majority believes in, even a majority of women. And to play the manly god I want to feel the manly god right in my face, you understand?

Dinah: Agreed, Abigal and Miriam?
(As both signal agreement ...) Then I ask the attorney to put forth all charges.

Abigal: I'll start at the very beginning of God's life, that is his creation of this world within six days, and within this creative process, at the sex issue. Your highness, why did you create first the male and then the female out of one of his ribs, as if small female body had to slot in big male's body?

Michal: Valid is the first creation account that says: And God created man in in the image of God, as man and woman. If you listen attentively you realize that I created them as man and woman because I am man and woman!

Abigal: Really, you are man and woman? Then tell us please how your female side could join in requiring Abraham to sacrifice his and Sarah's son?

82

Michal: Ask the priest who invented this sacrifice story.

Abigal: And tell us how a half-female God could order the angel of death to walk through Egypt and kill all firstborn sons of the Egyptian women?

Michal: Where is this horror story written?

Abigal: In the Second Book of Moses.

Michal: So ask Moses.

Abigal: I ask you why another prophet could quote you as follows: Thus said the Lord of Hosts: "I am exacting the penalty for what Amalek did to Israel some centuries ago. Now go, attack Amalek and proscribe all that belongs to him. Spare no one, but kill alike men and women, infants and sucklings, oxen and sheep, camels and asses!" End of quote! [1 Sm 15:2]

Miriam: This is a defamation of my client by a scribe named Samuel.

Abigal: Your Highness, did this order to murder women and children come from your mouth?

Michal: In all those cases where a silverback claims to have heard my voice you should check him in which voice God spoke to him and ask him to imitate this voice. And you may rest assured it was the dark threatful bass of an old male lion (she imitates) resounding in the prophet's empty cranium: Now go, attack Amalek and spare no one, but kill alike men and women, infants and sucklings, oxen and sheep, camels and asses!"

Dinah: So you say that the male scribes have distorted, predatorized and masculinized your image while in reality you are quite different?

Michal: As different as men and women.

Abigal: So Moses didn't speak in your name when he after the revenge raid against the Midianites gave the following order? "Now kill all the boys among the little ones, and every woman who has had sexual relations with a man. But all the young girls who are virgins, spare for yourselves." [Num 31:14-18]

Michal: Genocide in my name? Only men could strike on such a blasphemous idea.

Dinah: So it is not in your name when the fifth book of Moses proclaims the following commandment? "And when the Lord your God delivers it into your hand, you shall put all its males to the sword. Only the women and the children and the animals and all that is in the city, all its spoil, you shall take as booty for yourself." [Dt 20, 13-14]

Michal: Cut down the men and take the women: Could a God demand such crimes?

Abigal: Book of Judges, chapter 21: "Go and strike the inhabitants of Jabesh-gilead with the edge of the sword; also the women and the little ones. This is what you are to do: Kill every male and every woman who is not a virgin." [Judges 21:10-11].

Michal: I repeat: All these are mannish texts, composed by mean old silverbacks. But even so: All virgin girls were left alive, and they conceived and they had children who maybe became your great-grandmothers.

Abigal: That means we maybe are the great-granddaughters from the semen of Jewish rapists?

Michal: Not maybe but very surely. And aren't men exactly as you, the daughters of violators, want them to be? Didn't you women create man in your favorite design, as strong guy, reliable protector and good in bed? No pussy, no sissy, but man simply? Didn't the daughter of King Saul, and Michal was her name, accept the hero David who had paid the bride price of two hundred genuine Philistine foreskins? [1 Sm 18, 26-27]
Or would you prefer a world completely void of male violence, that is, completely void of men?
Or no world at all?
Do you charge me for having made this world? Would nonbeing be better than to be?

Dinah: That's not the question here to ask.

Michal: Of course it is. And I, as your creator, verily I say to you, I know a young woman who once gave a ruling on her baby's sheer existence – by abortion! For this child there is no world, is there? For this child there's never nothing because this young pregnant one determined: No, she said, never could I be mother, fate, creator of another human being! No, never shall another girl have to live through what I had to live through, defilement! No! Thus it raged and roared inside me, it must not be that this thing happens to her, to you, to me! And now, the stupid play is over! I am not able to play God, neither the father nor the mother! (She takes down the beard) Thanks be to God that I got rid of it!

Dinah: Please, Michal, you are the best one in this role. Please try it, without beard.

Michal: Shall I really? So I will try, without beard and without frills, to get an answer from each one of you: Isn't it better for my daughter, that I didn't abandon her in this world of rapers? And in a general way: Wouldn't this world better never have existed? Better never have existed anything? No stage, no play, no company, no audience? Wouldn't God have better aborted this world when she was pregnant with? Tell me just one reason why it was good that she gave birth to this world. Just one reason! I'm gonna count to three! I am God, ain't I? Let there be light, I said, and therefore now I can say "Let there be nothing", and in a moment nothing more exists and never anything existed. And if *you* by three have still not found a reason why this world should be, it won't be any more because the goddess spoke and not for joke, she broke the yoke and one two three, now you are free. Is that what you desire, that everything ends? No problem, as long as I am God. Agreed? Reflect it quickly, I count to three!

Abigal: Michal, have you lost all your courage?

Michal: One ...

Dinah: She lost her child.

Michal: Two ...

85

Abigal: No more – and by a word of God we end the heartache, and the thousand natural shocks that flesh is heir to. Finally we will be free ...

Michal: And two plus one makes ...

Miriam: Four! We are four, and listen, God! You didn't ask us when you made this world. You now don't have the right to abort it without asking us. And all of us! Also the child in my womb. Who knows what my son is up to do? Who knows why he intends to come?

Abigal: Exactly. Destruction is not a creative solution. With this destruction farce, Your Highness, you just want to distract us from the fact that you don't have any answers to our questions and complaints, as little as the Holy Books that tell us about you; those books flown from the pens of bunches of old bearded priests and prophets. Only men make laws. Only men become judges. This trial here is something never to occur on this men's playground. Out of touch with men's reality.
But the judgement we will pass is valid for reality, for the well-known reality that Roman men are practising the rape of Jewish girls as strategy to undermine the rebellious people. If thousands of young girls' wombs present us with sons of Rome while our men just look on helplessly, then women have to find a creative solution.

Michal: Eventually you see reason, as is proper for my creatures. For the creatures of a God who changes, who is capable of learning, a God who spoke to Moses from the burning bush: "I will be what I will be."

Abigal: You want to say that you're a God who changes with the change of times?

Michal: Of course. As I am not a figure carved from dry wood or barren stone, I am of life, and living is becoming, changing, responding to ever new situations.
Did I respond to Moses out of the burning bush proclaiming in a dark and raucous roaring voice: I am the Almighty?
No, because might is the contrary of right.
Did I say that I'm all-knowing?

86

No, because if we are free nobody knows what will come out.

Did I say that I'm the greatest?

No, because this greatest thing is men's obsession.

So please just memorize the rule of three: God is the contrary of omnipotence, of infinite wisdom, of grandeur. God is powerless, small and learning. In short, she is a child.

God is the child in Miriam's womb.

And listen what this child is saying: I want to live. I want you to accept me and protect me. Ain't I entitled to?

And now you must change something, girls! Cut off the beard and care for a creative solution!

Abigal: The court retires for deliberation.

(Abigal, Dinah and Miriam confer in the background, while Michal paces up and down the apron).

Michal: Creative solution? What could that be? Perhaps I should just ask my intelligent creatures? Just ask the audience having been all eyes on our absurd trial. How should three females find a creative solution for the definitely male problem of strategic rape? No idea? That's what I surmised. And wanna bet? Two thousand years from now this mannish disease will not be cured, try me! How I would like to ask our great-granddaughters thousand or two-thousand years from now if they still know what rape is! If soldiers still are saying that the losers' women are the winners' fun? And whether God still helps the strong ones and whether he still wears a beard and smells of frankincense, or he became a child already.

A creative solution, what could that be?

Abigal: And now we go, blow upon blow.

(She knocks her tin mug on the bench three times).

We pronounce the sentence.

First, if God is almighty and all-knowing, he is guilty of denial of assistance towards young women and their violently sired children.

Second, however, God is, as we heard here from her own mouth, actually much more an entity as powerless and small and needing protection as a child. Therefore our judgement has to start out from the child that God is.

Hence, as an urgent measure, the law defining Jewish affiliation needs to be changed. In the first sentence, stating that Jewish is who descends from a Jewish father, the word father will be cancelled and replaced by mother. Thus it will be guaranteed that all those children who come into being by Roman rape belong to us nevertheless. Valid is from now on that Jewish is whoever has a Jewish mother. The father doesn't matter.

Third: The defendant is sentenced to assume his fatherhood for all – I repeat: for all and every single one of these children. Anyone of those rape-sired sons of Roman fathers has the right to call himself a Son of God or more precisely, in Aramaic language, a Son of the Father, a Bar Abbas. The sentence is pronounced, the trial finished!

Michal: Fatherhood for all those children! Father in heaven, please assume! All Barei Abbas are now your sons! Abigal, you outdid yourself with this punch line at the end of this trial.

Dinah: Michal, I think you got it wrong. This wasn't play. This is reality. If we don't acknowledge those legions of sons of legionaries as our own by rating them as Sons of Our Father ...

Abigal: ... then the Romans would have won not only by their warriors, but by our wombs as well.

Dinah: You said it. Miriam, your child will be a Son of God.

Michal: Or Her daughter.

Miriam: He will be a son, I feel it. I know it. A son he's gonna be, a vigorous son, but no Panthera! Neither meat nor females he will eat. Instead, a grandly rabbi he will be, pronouncing justice for us women.

Abigal: Yes he will!

Miriam: And he will place the children in the center and he will say: you have to turn and to become like children, feel like children who are not guilty of what adults use to do to them.

Abigal: A rabbi for women, sinners and children. And Bar Abbas they will call him, Rabbi Bar Abbas!

Miriam: Rabbi Son of Father, of a father who will not subjugate nor sacrifice but liberate.

Dinah: All sacrifice he will abolish, beginning with the animals in temple!

Miriam: The pigeons he will set free from the cages, and the tables of the pigeon-sellers he will overthrow. And then, and then he will expel the Romans from Jerusalem, all the Pantheras Legioneras, and like a herd of pigs they will rush down into the sea and drown in the water ...

Dinah: But pigs can swim ...

Michal: Woe be to the rapers! He will drown them like the Egyptians in the Sea of Reeds! The son of Miriam will be my anointed one, anointed with the finest oil of nards by the hands of this sinful woman who aborted. By my anointment the son of Miriam will be our Messiah, and he in turn will justify the sinful woman.

Dinah: Messiah? Rather don't you aim so high.

Miriam: Yeshua I will call my son, for he will fight the Romans and he will stand on the mount of olives and God will help us in the battle.

Dinah: Yeshua? Listen, Miriam. Yeshua is quite nice. But nicer would be Yitzisha, Smile Woman. Think about it, Miriam!

Miriam: Yitzisha? You're funny, Dinah.

Dinah: Funny was the yiddishe mame who said: I will name my son in honor of my father. I will call him Grandpa.

Abigal: Women are that stupid. You know why Solomon was a wise man? It's simple: He had thousand wives and never time to consult just one of them.

Dinah: Was that a smile on your face, Miriam?

Miriam: I didn't smile. Yeshua chuckled about the Grandpa. Feel my belly, he still giggles.

Dinah: By the way, what's the name of the grandpa of your Joseph?

Miriam: Jacob.

Dinah: So Jacob will be the name of your next son.

Miriam: My next son?

Abigal: And your first daughter Salome will be wiser than Solomon.

Dinah: But now you smiled, admit it!

Miriam: Yeshua did. And now ... I feel ... He's kicking inside, he's pushing me ... I think he wants to come out to this funny world ...

Dinah: The first contractions? Abigal, please help me ...

6th Scene: Delivery

Abigal and Dinah bring Miriam to bed (behind the background), while Michal steps forward to the apron.

Michal: No. Nuts, simply nuts. A nutty play. Never will I anoint a man, and much less the Messiah who will never come. I prefer to be the sinful woman who aborted. I prefer not to throw children into this world where rapers fuck you and Romans crucify you.
I don't abandon children on this earth. I did abort this baby and I adhere to what I've done. I'm even somewhat glad about it. It's been the baby of this Roman swine, not mine, not mine!
Not mine has been the baby I simply could not stay with. My child, my child, you hear me, my child? You rest in peace secure, salvaged in the cozy warmness of the nothing. Sleep deeply and no one will

awaken you. No one will torture you, no one will rape you and never you will croak on cross.

Michal starts to sing to the melody of "Unter di khurves fun poyln".

Michal: Safe in the earth you are sleeping
baby mine and not mine
in cozy womb, there's no weeping
never reason to whine.
No unrest, no fussing in the womb of nothing.

Safe in the earth you are hiding,
never a seeker will come,
no wolf, no lion, no panther
no God and also no mum.
No unrest, no fussing in the womb of nothing.

Over you flowers blossom,
fondled by breezes so mild.
Now you no mame will fondle,
your mame has no child.
No unrest, no fussing in the womb of nothing.

(At this point the baby is heard screaming the first time)

Over the flowers a blackbird
flutters fearful around
Maybe she's losing her nestlings?
My baby I never found.
Sleep my son forever, sleep, you have been never.

(Dinah puts the newborn baby in Michal's arms and keeps standing next to her. Abigal and eventually Miriam join).

Abigal: And the Queen of Shaba came to see the newborn son, and she brought him sundry toys (she shakes the rattle) ...

Dinah: And the wise old woman from the orient followed the morning star and found the baby before noon and on his mother's face she found a faint but charming smile.

Michal: And the childless one forgot her retrospection and her rage and looked at the child for quite some time and mused about what was written on his forehead and which role he'd go to play one day.

(With Abigal, Dinah and Michal humming the melody, Miriam speaks ...)

Miriam: And the mother said delivery was easy.
My son didn't come like a brickstone
and not like a rock by any means,
but still he'll be a cornerstone.

7th Scene: Interaction with the audience

This interaction is an important and integral part of Miriam's Midwives. Unscripted in its outcome, it nevertheless may be prepared and guided by placing incognito actors (or challenging troublemakers) in the audience.
The following is meant but as suggestion.

Dinah: (Steps forward) Miriam's last word *cornerstone* completes this odd play, so far away from all those nativity plays we are accustomed to since our childhood. Considering the scandalous blasphemies against the Holy Virgin and the Lord of Hosts put forth during this play by unholy women, we now invite the audience to give full scope to their more than justified anger.

Abigal: That means we appoint you as the jury judging our play, and we are now the defendants.
Michal: In order that the debate will not go wild, and also to make you feel freer to speak out, we have prepared some theses and also engaged three representants of different camps ...
Abigal: But we'd like to start with a warming up in form of a very general and informal opinion poll. You know that in democracy each one has the right to join a safe majority. So during the following balloting please check how many hands are up already and then join.

First scaling: We will propose 12 attributes, and you may vote for as many as you want except the first three: Do you think the play was (1) good – (2) average – (3) bad?

Do you regard it (4) interesting – (5) blasphemous – (6) outrageous – (7) devilish – (8) human – (9) inspiring – (10) dull – (11) destructive or – (12) touching?

In the second scaling we propose but one thesis you may agree with or refute. Our thesis is: Living together in a pluralistic society requires a certain measure of respect for differing religious views [keywords for instance: Charly Hebdo, Burkini ...] Has this necessary minimum of respect been abided by our play? Please vote yes – no – undecided.

Dinah: If these questions remind you all too much on Punch-and-Judy-theatre, we appreciate. But please consider also, that Goethe's famous drama of Doctor Faustus and his pregnant Gretchen started from a German county fair puppet theater. And the famous question Gretchen asked her lover Doctor Faustus was: What's your stance as to religion?

Referring to our Punch-and-Jewess-theatre, I as Gretchen would like to ask you now: Is this play rather religious or anti-religious?

Should this play be enacted by theaters which receive taxpayer support in any form, yes or no?

Miriam: At this point we ask you to give us space to plead in our defense, particularly against the possible charges that this play is blasphemous, irreverent toward Jesus, Mary, Joseph and also inappropriate for children.

(Suggestion: **Abigal** pleads ad Jesus, **Dinah** ad Joseph, **Michal** ad God, using the corresponding theses from the postface. Then Miriam takes the floor again):

Miriam: Now we come to our theses, the theses [of the play's author and] of this female group of theatre. Please break in at any point.

1. Our first thesis refers to my role as Miriam: I assert that this play shows not lesser, but much more respect to Miriam of Nazareth than the Christian tradition of a Mother of God who principally, and that is from first to last, from conception to the crucifixion of her son, is restricted to the passively obedient role women should play in society.

2. My second thesis refers to my son who stands in the center of our play though he doesn't enter scene himself. I assert that our play shows incomparably more respect also to Jesus than the Christian tradition of a passive victim, a child of sacrifice sired by a divine father with an earthly mother who was betrothed to a honest man, divinely sired exactly for the purpose of his later getting sacrificed.

3. And my third thesis states: This nativity play conveys a humanely comprehensible explanation of the fact that this birth was the beginning of a life whose end is the subject of Passion Plays; of Passion Plays that often triggered anti-Jewish pogroms. In brief, the violence of the outset was followed by the violence of the end and the violence of revenge for a cruel murder that not the Jews committed, but the Jews were punished for during two millennia.

Michal: Does this desire for just punishment arise from the very natural compassion of children – and we all are grown-up children – with the innocent son of Miriam, who allegedly was betrayed by Judas, condemned by Jews and crucified at the behest of Jews? And how does it affect children when the Christ child who at Christmas lies in the manger dies on cross before Easter, and so on year after year? Of course our drama is absolutely inappropriate for children. But isn't any Nativity Play, with or without the murderous perfidious King Herod, also the first act to a Passion Play? Will children with their highly sensitive antennae not perceive this link and what this manger child is destined for? Haven't children the right to be spared of pictures and narratives which are appropriate for learning to hate people of other religions?

Abigal: We will not ask you what you think about our performance as actresses. Much more important is for instance the question whether rape should be or can be presented on a stage at all. Holocaust survivor Ruth Klüger said that the narrative of a torture – and rape is torture – that the telling of a torture levels down the terror of the mute and speechless victim. Is it possible to play the tongue-tied being at the mercy of a rapist?

Miriam: Maybe that's impossible but necessary nonetheless? The American traumatologist Yael Danieli writes: "What is not spoken about cannot come to rest. And if it doesn't come to rest it will continue festering, from generation to generation."

94

Michal: We'll now present some theses that can not be answered with a Yes or No and also not with good – average – bad, but that should animate your personal taking a stand. The personal opinion of every single spectator of our play is sought also when we now invite three women from different political-religious directions to take a seat on stage to form up here a core room of our debate. We welcome ...

(The three representants take their seats on the stage).

Dinah: 1. Again this one: Is this play religious or anti-religious?
2. This play's composition is due very vitally to the works of the feminist theologian and former nun Jane Schaberg. In her obituary posted on a progressive Catholic website on April 18, 2012, Kathy Schiffer wrote: "Jane Schaberg died last night at her home, in the company of friends." After recalling the hostilities Professor Jane Schaberg had passed through, Kathy Schiffer concludes with "Whatever she thought and taught about Jesus, about His Mother and about His Church, Jane knows now. May God in His infinite mercy show her Himself as He truly is. May her soul, and the souls of all the faithful departed, through the mercy of God rest in peace. Amen."
This sounds as if little Jane had strained His great mercy badly. But one Dr.Tee was much more severe, writing that "The Bible teaches that 'anyone who brings a different gospel than the one Jesus and His disciples brought were accursed.' ... If this woman had truly repented before her death then she probably would have received mercy and salvation. Now it is too late."
Jane Schaberg's guilt was grave, as one woman named Maggy Goff commented shortly: "How many did she lead astray?" One *Sue from Buffalo* however didn't agree with Dr.Tee that it's too late for Jane, because she wrote: "No one knows whether or not she truly repented before her death. She could have raised her eyes to the heavens and spoke the words 'Jesus, have mercy' in that split second before death."
Apparently here two very different views of God are colliding. Will we four women have to repent for this play timely?
3. Our play builds mainly on Jane Schaberg's thesis that Miriam of Nazareth conceived her son Jesus in an act of violence, being raped by a Roman soldier, and that this terribly violent and impure beginning paradoxically "presents us with fuller human realities and there-

fore with deeper theological potential" than the belief in a virginal conception from God.

4. If you would now be asked to write a very short afterword to our play, what would you deem most important?
What would change if the Christian Churches adopted the standpoint of Jane Schaberg? Would Christendom break down or rather became more true to the intentions of Jesus?

Abigal: Brazilian theater maker Augusto Boal, himself victim of the violent Brazilian military dictatorship from 1974-1995, is famous for his *Theatre of the Oppressed*. In his workshops, Boal used to encourage spectators to reenact the play in a different way, particularly with a different end in a way that conflicts get visible or may be resolved. That's difficult in our play, but maybe you have suggestions what should be played in a different way or with additional roles? We are open to any propositions except that Miriam should marry her rapist.

Michal: Most important is that you at the end of this play feel free to speak out your own thoughts, critique and opinion ...

Dinah: Thanks for your applause and your critique, your civilized non-violent discussion concerning Miriam and the Midwives.
In honor of Jane Schaberg, we finish with an obit written by Shula Fleischer ... (see next page)

Performing rights
... are granted free of royalties and independent of place and number of presentations, provided that ten percent of the earnings are given to accredited eligible projects in the following areas: Human rights of women, children, minorities; intercultural and interfaith rapprochement (topically fitting: Palestine-Israel), ecology, environment and animal rights.

Contact
konrig@t-online.de
kyriggenmann@gmail.com
facebook, Konrad Yona Riggenmann

C Postface

Jane Schaberg,
in memoriam

Farewell to a forward thinker by Shula Fleischer, April 18, 2012

Jane was a true scholar and an amazing researcher. She did not take her writings lightly, and her work should not be considered blasphemy. Please reserve judgement until you have read her books. Only then you can appreciate or dispute her conclusions.

Jane was the kindest human being, taking in children who lived on 12th street in Detroit and giving them an opportunity of an education and exposure to a better life, which their parents could not have done for them.

Jane was kind to animals and found beauty in all of God's creatures even in those deformed and handicapped that most of us would have long walked away from.

In my eyes she merits to sit right next to God. I personally lost a mentor, a colleague and a very dear friend.

May her memory be a blessing!

What can I, K.Y. Riggenmann, add to this obit? Just my hope that Jane Schaberg would applaud to Miriam's Midwives and boos would come from those people who let her automobile go up in flames (the Detroit way of auto-da-fé).

You, dear reader, can judge now: Are Miriam's Midwives blasphemous, an affront, irreverent towards Jesus, God, Mary and the candle-rich holiday that shines into our childhood?

My first play of theatre was a Swabian Nativity Play that was praised as child-oriented, humanely touching and down-to-earth. I'll try to prove that these three attributes also apply to my current drama for four women, and that it is just the contrary of blasphemous, inept and irreverent, especially towards four persons, plus the children.

1. Jesus: What would be so bad if he'd been born not in a stable and not been put into the manger between ox and donkey but had been begotten in deepest humiliation of his mother?

If the dignity of the powerless to him would have been not just a moral demand but a built-in part of his body, this abused body which today adorns in wood-carved version all corners of this planet?

And if his incarnation is being interpreted theologically as a voluntary, extreme act of self-humiliation, as the descent of the Son of the Most High into the deepest suffering of human nature: How could this descent be deepest-possible if his conception had not been an extremely violent act of (in)human baseness?

2. Joseph: A young man, probably anti-Roman rebel, who adopts the rape-sired Roman son of his fiancée as his own son: is he lesser apt for sanctity than the post-sexual old man displayed on Mary's side by generations of Christian painters?

3. Mary: Does it any harm to Mary's holiness to assume that motherhood had not been announced to her by an angel but enforced on her by a rapist? Which woman should weigh as more holy, more whole, more healing: One who incorporates the divine semen meekly and accepts the resulting child submissively, knowing that the little rascal is godly – or one who accepts the offspring of her rapist nonetheless with love and rears him with kindness during twenty years without being able to forget just one day that one day?

4. **God**: Does it any harm to the God of Jesus that the Messiah Son of David arose not only from the incest of Judah with Tamar, not only from the harlot womb of Rahab, from the line of Moabite seductress Ruth and from the adultery of David with Bathseba but moreover from the rape of hitherto blameless virgin Mary? Does it devalue Jesus' unusual support for children, women, sinners if it has to do with his own biography?

And isn't his so awfully impure conception by violence at least much more probable than the presumption that the Almighty created this one sperm cell out of nothing and brought it into one of Mary's egg cells just as miraculously? The latter case would leave me with the question whether Jesus, who taught mankind the Our Father prayer, was a first class son of Our Father and we but second sons or, even worse, just Our Father's further daughters? Or why, if the Almighty can sire sons and daughters so effortless and easily – why not ever and always, so we could refrain from sinful sex?

On the subject of: Is it so honorable for Our Father to be on a level with the child-rich Roman womanizer Jupiter by siring a son with the fiancée of a Jewish carpenter?

May we compare Our Father with this just ersatz father Joseph who adopted the howsoever sired boy because he was "a righteous man and did not want to disgrace her publicly" (Matthew 1:19)? Our Father is righteous too, right? Or didn't Abraham rightly ask Him: "Should not the Judge of all the earth do what is right?" If yes, how could a righteous God even consider not accepting the son of Panthera as his own son, as Josef did?

And one last question, asked by the former Catholic seminarist that I am: According to Catholic moral doctrine, an act of sexual love, in order to be sinless, must always contain at least a minimal chance for its natural purpose, the siring of a child. So doesn't hold also the reverse that any siring must contain sexual love? Did God take to heart this in the case of Mary?

5. Last not least, the children: No, of course the play of Miriam's Midwives is no child's play, inapt for any stage between kindergarten and college. But also nativity plays with Christ Child, shepherds and three kings are highly questionable as children's theater. Not for the massacre Betlehem's children suffered in his place but because the wooden manger every year before Easter becomes the wooden cross he was destined for by his heavenly father, right?

Not for no reason Jewish psychologist Erik Eriksson called Christendom a "religion of adults". Rather because children have highly sensitive antennae ...

Curitiba, October 25, 2018   Konrad Yona Riggenmann

99

Bibliography

Alberti, Bettina: Die Seele fühlt von Anfang an. Wie pränatale Erfahrungen unsere Beziehungsfähigkeit prägen. München 2005.

Arad, Yitzchak (ed.): The Pictorial History of the Holocaust. Yadvashem, Jerusalem 1990.

Aslan, Reza; Zealot. The Life and Times of Jesus of Nazareth. New York 2013.

Ben-Chorin, Shalom: Paulus. Der Völkerapostel in jüdischer Sicht. Munich 1980.

Bonder, Nilton: A Alma Imoral. Rio de Janeiro 1998.

Capps, Donald: The Child's Song. Religious Abuse of Children. Louisville, Kentucky 1995.

Callsen, Brigitta et al. (Fritz Peter Knapp, Manuela Niesner and Martin Przybilski): Das jüdische Leben Jesu, Toldot Jeschu. Die älteste lateinische Übersetzung in den Falsitates Judaeorum von Thomas Ebendorfer. Vienna and Munich 2003.

Carroll, James: Constantine's Sword. The Church and the Jews. Boston and New York 2001.

Cohn, Haim: O Julgamento e a Morte de Jesus. Rio de Janeiro 1994 (German edition: Cohn, Chaim: Der Prozeß und Tod Jesu aus jüdischer Sicht, Frankfurt am Main 1997).

Crossan, John Dominic: Who killed Jesus? New York 1996.

de Rosa, Peter: Der Jesus-Mythos. Über die Krise der katholischen Kirche. Munich 1993.

Durant, Will: Caesar und Christus. Eine Kulturgeschichte Roms und des Christentums von den Anfängen bis zum Jahr 325 n.Chr. Bern 1949.

Eisler, Robert: Man Into Wolf. An Anthropological Interpretation of Sadism, Masochism and Lycanthropy. London 1951.

Ellis, Marc: Unholy Alliance: Religion and Atrocity in Our Time. Minneapolis 1997.

Ferenczi, Sandor: Schriften zur Psychoanalyse II, Frankfurt/M.1972.

Flusser, David: Jesus in Selbstzeugnissen und Bilddokumenten. Reinbek 1968.

Fricke, Weddig: Standrechtlich gekreuzigt. Person und Prozeß des Jesus aus Galiläa. Reinbek 1991.

Freire, Paulo: Pädagogik der Unterdrückten. Reinbek 1991.

Freud, Sigmund: O Mal-Estar na Civilização [Civilization and Its Discontents]. Obras completas, volume 18. São Paulo 2010.

Greenberg, Irving: The Jewish Way. Living the Holidays. New York 1993.

Häsing, Helga and **Janus**, Ludwig: Ungewollte Kinder. Annäherungen, Beispiele, Hilfen. Reinbek 1994.

Heer, Friedrich: Gottes erste Liebe. Die Juden im Spannungsfeld der Geschichte. Berlin 1981.

Horsley, Richard A. and **Silberman**, Neil Asher: The Message and the Kingdom. How Jesus and Paul Ignited a Revolution and Transformed the Ancient World. New York 1997.

Isaac, Jules: Jesus und Israel. Vienna and Zurich 1968.

Janus, Ludwig: Wie die Seele entsteht. Heidelberg 1997.

Janus, Ludwig: Der Seelenraum des Ungeborenen. Pränatale Psychologie und Therapie. Düsseldorf and Zurich 2000.

Josephus, Flavius: Geschichte des Jüdischen Krieges, Wiesbaden 1982.

Kertész, Imre: Kaddisch für ein nicht geborenes Kind. Reinbek 2002.

Klausner, Joseph: Jesus von Nazareth. Jerusalem 1952.

Lanzmann, Claude: Shoah. Düsseldorf 1986.

Lapide, Pinchas: Der Rabbi von Nazareth. Wandlungen des jüdischen Jesusbildes. Trier 1974.

Lapide, Pinchas: Er wandelte nicht auf dem Meer. Ein jüdischer Theologe liest die Evangelien. Gütersloh 1984.

Lapide, Pinchas: Wer war schuld an Jesu Tod? Gütersloh 1987.

Lapide, Pinchas: Warum kommt er nicht? Gütersloh 1988.

Lehmann, Johannes: Das Geheimnis des Rabbi Jesus. Die Wahrheit von Qumran und was Urchristen und Kirche daraus machten. Hamburg 1993.

Levend, Helga / **Janus**, Ludwig (ed): Drum hab ich kein Gesicht. Kinder aus unerwünschten Schwangerschaften. Würzburg 2000.

Lüdemann, Gerd: Jesus nach 2000 Jahren. Was er wirklich sagte und tat. Lüneburg 2000.

Maccoby, Hyam: Judas Iscariot and the Myth of Jewish Evil. New York 1992.

Maccoby, Hyam: Jesus und der Jüdische Freiheitskampf. Freiburg i.Br. 1996.

Michael, Robert: Holy Hatred. Christian Antisemitism and the Holocaust. New York 2006.

Nicholls, William: Christian Antisemitism. A History of Hate. Lanham (Maryland) 2004.

Sartre, Jean-Paul: Bariona oder Der Sohn des Donners. Reinbek 2013.

Schaberg, Jane: The Illegitimacy of Jesus. A Feminist Theological Interpretation of the Infancy Narratives. San Francisco, ca. 1994.

Schoeps, Hans-Joachim: Jewish Christianity: Factional Disputes in the Early Church. Philadelphia 1969.

Schützenberger, Anne Ancelin, in: The Ancestor Syndrome. Trans-generational Psychotherapy and the Hidden Link in the Family Tree. New York 1998.

Schwab, Gabriele: Haunting Legacies. Violent Histories and Trans-generational Trauma. New York 2010.

Schweitzer, Albert: Die psychiatrische Beurteilung Jesu. Hildesheim, Zurich, New York 2005.

Szondi, Leopold: Schicksalsanalyse. Wahl in Liebe, Freundschaft, Beruf, Krankheit und Tod. Basel 2004.

Tabor, James D.: Die Jesus-Dynastie. Das verborgene Leben von Jesus und seiner Familie und der Ursprung des Christentums. Munich 2007.

Telushkin, Joseph: Jewish Literacy. The most important things to know about the Jewish religion, its people, and its history. New York 2001.

Travers Herford, Robert: Christianity in Talmud and Midrash. London 1903; reprint 2012 (forgottenbooks).

Van der Kolk, Bessel: The Body Keeps the Score. Brain, Mind and Body in the Healing of Trauma. New York 2014.

Weiss, John: Ideology of Death. Why the Holocaust Happened in Germany. Chicago 1997.

Zimmermann, Béatrice Acklin and **Annen**, Franz: Versöhnt durch den Opfertod Christi? Die christliche Sühneopfertheologie auf der Anklagebank. Zurich 2009.

Bible editions used:

Arenhoevel, Diego (ed.): Jerusalemer Bibel. Freiburg, Basel and Vienna 1968.

Biblehub.com.

Jewish Publication Society: Hebrew-English Tanach. Philadelphia 1999.

Levine, Amy-Jill / **Brettler**, Marc Zvi (editors): The Jewish Anno-tated New Testament. Oxford 2011.

Pictures

Cover: Lorenzo Lotto (1480-1557), Natívitá: Wikimedia Commons. Jewish woman abused by Ukrainian Mob (entire picture: p.3): Arad, p.176, courtesy Yadvashem Archives.

p.4: Madonna of the Yarnwinder, Museum Mexico-City: Wikimedia Commons.

p.16: Nazareth, painted by Scottish artist David Roberts in 1842: Wikimedia Commons.

p.19: Virginis partus, from the Hortus Deliciarium of Abbess Herrad of Landsberg: Wikimedia Commons.

p.32: Tombstones Panthera and Pintaius:
a) Photos: Wikipedia; (keywords Panthera/Signifer)
b) Drawing: Flusser, p.40, courtesy Rowohlt Verlag Reinbek.

p.47: James Tissot (1836-1902), Barabbas: Wikimedia Commons.

p.61: Spindles: Wikipedia.

p.97: Jane Schaberg: Courtesy Patheos.com; patheos.com/blogs/kathyschiffer/2012/04/jane-schaberg-feminist-theologian-has-died.

Song   "Unter di khurves fun poyln"

Lyrics: Manger, Itzig: (1911-1969): Dunkelgold. Gedichte jiddisch und deutsch. Frankfurt on Main 2004.

Music: Shoul Beresowsky (1908-1975).

On CDs: Jalda Rebling, Stefan Maass, Hans-Werner Apel: Die goldene Pawe. Jiddische Lieder (raumklang.de, 1996). Daniel Kahn and The Painted Bird: The Broken Tongue. (paintedbird.de, 2006).

Sheet music for **"Unter di khurves fun poyln"**
"To the house of our Miriam"
"Safe in the earth you are sleeping"

The author of this play notated this music sheet by ear, in gratitude to Itzig Manger and Shoul Beresowsky.